Presented to:

_____

From:

_____

Date:

_____

Thrust
Into
The Fire

Brad Gillman

Copyright 2012 – Brad Gillman

All rights reserved. This book is protected by the copyright laws of the United States of America. This book may not be copied or reprinted for commercial gain or profit. The use of short quotations or occasional page copying for personal or group study is permitted and encouraged. Permission will be granted upon request. Unless otherwise noted, Scripture quotations are from the New King James Version, Copyright 1982 by Thomas Nelson, Inc. Scripture quotations marked NLT are taken from the Holy Bible, New Living Translation, copyright 1996, 2004. Used by permission of Tyndale House Publishers, Wheaton, IL 60189. All rights reserved. Please note that Legacy Media Group's publishing style capitalizes certain pronouns in Scripture that refer to the Father, Son, and Holy Spirit, and may differ from some publisher's styles. Take note that any mention of satan and related names are not capitalized. We choose not to acknowledge him, even to the point of violating grammatical rules.

Legacy Media Group Publishers
ISBN-13: 978-1478220718
ISBN-10: 1478220716

Dedication

I want to dedicate this book to my wife, Alice Gillman, and to my mom, Sandy Gillman. Without these two special women in my life, this book would not be possible.

To Alice: Your steadfast love and belief in me has not wavered. I thank you for your support and constant love. You have enriched my life in ways so much stronger than words can express. I love you more and more every day and look forward to an awesome future with you as we walk together and discover all the Lord has for us. Thank you for being my best friend and partner in this walk with the Lord!

To Mom: Thank you for always believing in me. Thank you for standing with me and encouraging me throughout my life. I appreciate the fact that you always went above and beyond the call of duty as a parent to see that I was always in a position to grow. Your support means so much to me.

With that being said, I dedicate *Thrust into the Fire* to both of you.

Acknowledgements

I would like to thank the following people for their encouragement and ministry as I have written this book:

My wife, Alice Gillman: For your unwavering support and love.

To Joshua Fowler: Your teaching, training, and fathering, played such a pivotal role in me writing this book.

To Charlie Coker: Your love, support, and belief in me, helped complete this book.

My friend Don Wacker: For always being there to help keep me on track.

My friend Bridget Zoltek: For helping me pull everything together into a completed work.

My friend Earl Hollister: For your friendship and encouragement.

My friend Allen Wilfong: For your prayers and praying with me at all hours of the day and night.

The HSGEM Board: For standing with me and helping see this project through to completion.

Special thanks goes to our ministry partners who made this book possible: Robin Smith, George Devitt, Earl Hollister, Jason Bagnell, Woody Folker, Alex Zanazanian, Bridget Zoltek, Tom, McElroy, Fred Fairchild, and Christine Jordan.

Endorsements

Christian testimonies are a powerful and effective means of communicating the truth. I recommend Brad's story to all believers who have lost their way. The world, the flesh and the devil will do all they can to keep you from experiencing God's best for your life. Brad's account of how he overcame will encourage you to do so as well. Thrust into the Fire will encourage you as you pray for your loved ones to come to the Lord and or rededicate their lives. Don't give up praying for them. They are not out of reach from God.

Joan Hunter
Author, Evangelist
President of Joan Hunter Ministries

I want to thank Brad for spending the time to share his story. The Lord reminded me of something as I read in 1 Corinthians 3:10-15. We can only build on Christ, and even as we build on Christ we need to beware of how we do it. All works of the flesh will burn, but every work of the Spirit shall be rewarded. Thanks Brad for reminding us of this.

Jeff Suttles, an Apostle of Jesus Christ
Lifehouse Ministries
Flat Rock, NC

In this book, "Thrust IntoThe Fire" Brad tells the story about his journey that unearths ancient Hebrew truth hidden from him, even though he was born and raised Jewish. God is in the process of restoring Kingdom mentality to the Church. I have had the privilege of becoming Brad's spiritual father at the same time we both were learning how to be Kingdom fathers and sons. As we helped each other work though father issues God has granted us the revelation of our true identity in Christ. This book gives you insight on how to let the fire of God burn off the old habits, all the while letting God preserve what is useful and needed to navigate this kingdom life that will manifest the sons of God.

Charles L. Coker Jr.
Senior Leader, One Kingdom Fellowship
Deltona. Florida

Do you feel like a missing piece of life's puzzle? Are you struggling to find acceptance and the reason of your existence? "Thrust into the Fire", is a textbook case of how one man, asking those same questions, found the answer to life's most sought after question; "Why am I here". Take a journey with Brad, as he faces life's struggles and worldly desires, and how he came face to face with the answer to his own search to that same question: "Why am I here?"

Eric Marshall,
Pastor of Warriors for Christ Training Center Church
Merritt Island, Florida

Thrust IntoThe Fire is a story that will inspire you. We need to be reminded that the Lord is in the transformation business. When the Father gets a hold of someone's heart He does extraordinary things. Brad's life and testimony reminds us that the Lord can find us anywhere and order our steps. Knowing Brad, I have the honor and privilege to know that the transformation by the Father is amazing. A life that finds itself looking for more in the midst of the corporate ladder is one that many people can identify with. Something that just gnaws at you but you can't put your finger on it. Then one day it hits you, you are being pursued by God. Many will benefit from this book as they read it and realize what is happening in their own life. They are being pursued and prepared to be thrust into the fire.

Louis DeSiena
Senior Leader
The Gate Fellowship

Thrust Into The Fire is a brutally honest and transparent revelation of Brad's spiritual journey. Every reader will be inspired by the incredible transformation from a life held captive in darkness and self-destruction to God's amazing grace that brought light, healing, and victory. There is nothing so powerful as the personal testimony of life that was burning in the fire of hell's torments only to be delivered by the wonderful cleansing fire of the Holy Spirit. Thrust Into the Fire is that testimony... He is worthy of all praise!

Pastor James Wiley
Oak Grove Church
Port St. Joe, FL

Table of Contents

Dedication 5
Acknowledgements 7
Endorsements 8
Foreword 13
1 - The American Dream 17
2 - Me, Myself, and the Devil! 27
3 - Climbing the Corporate Ladder 39
4 - Jesus? Are You For Real? 51
5 - The Calling 61
6 - Bibles, Bibles, & More Bibles 73
7 - The Airport Anointing 83
8 - Chasing The Holy Ghost 95
9 - California Dreaming 107
10 - Speak Lord! Your Servant Is Listening!. 119
11 - Triumphant Faith 131
12: The Benjamin Blessing........................... 143
About The Author 152

Foreword

Brad Gillman is a man who went from trying to burn a bible to burning with passion for God. He's been raised up as a Harvester and Fire Starter for the Kingdom of God. As you read his testimony I believe you, too, will be set ablaze.

Brad's testimony will stir a greater hunger in you for the Presence of God and cause you to run with feet of fire to help gather in the harvest of souls. Your family, friends and co-workers are in for it, because as you read you will receive an impartation that will help you bring transformation to their lives.

Brad's simple and no nonsense approach in sharing the Gospel is sure to reach both those who are unsaved and those who are tired of religion. Proverbs 11:30 says, "He that wins souls is wise". I recommend that you gift additional copies to everyone you know who needs the Lord and anyone who has a passion to win souls.

I personally have witnessed Brad Gillman's genuine love for God and people. He is more than an author; he's a practitioner. He truly lives what he preaches. Brad has a heart of a servant and a worshipper.

I can say without reservation that your life will be enriched as you read this book. So buckle up and get ready for the ride of your life as you go on this journey with Brad in Thrust into the Fire.

Dr. Joshua Fowler
Author of Governors of Praise, Access Granted and I.D. Required
Senior Leader of LegacyLife.org & GodDay.com
Orlando, FL

Introduction

On January 7, 2007, I came to know Jesus Christ as my Lord and Savior. The 33 years before this happened were tumultuous and filled with a life of sex, drugs, and rock and roll. The title of this book has many meanings. For most of my adult life I was thrust into the fire of Hell; but all that changed the moment I allowed Jesus Christ to transform my life. At that point, a shift took place, and I was thrust into the fire of God. *Thrust into the Fire* is my testimony. It's the story of how Jesus took a Jewish boy and called him home.

From a young age I always wondered if Jesus was real. In the weeks before my salvation, I felt I was losing everything...my wife, my family, my company, my house, my vehicles. I was alone and without hope. I had nowhere else to turn and reached a personal lifetime low.

My heart in writing this book is for you to realize that you are not alone! I want you to know that others have experienced the same pain, hurt and loss that you may be experiencing. I want you to know that you do have a place to turn. You do have a hand to hold. You do have a listening ear. You do have a provider and a deliverer. He brings hope to the hopeless and strength to the powerless. His name is Jesus!

Come with me on this journey and let me show you how I was *Thrust into the Fire!*

1 - The American Dream

What does happiness mean to you? Where does true happiness and joy come from? Have you ever tried to fill the void within you with "stuff"? From a young age, I always wanted "The American Dream." I wanted the fantasy life that I constantly saw on television. I selfishly envisioned myself in a beautiful five bedroom, three bathroom house with a pool, a three car garage, and a white picket fence. I expected that I would have a Lincoln Navigator for my wife to drive, a Lexus LS400 for myself and, of course, a Corvette for the weekend. I expected to have two children: one boy and one girl who were two years apart so they could be raised together. And let's not forget about my Master Craft ski boat and Harley Davidson Road King!

After hunting the American dream for so long I found it important to share with you the truth that I discovered. This is a story about my life: the good, the bad, and the ugly. I hope that my story inspires you to seek the truth. Why do I say 'seek the truth?' Well, I believe we are being lied to in America about the "American Dream." Why would I say something like that? Am I saying it to get your attention or do I really feel that way? The

The American Dream

American Dream that is pitched to us centers all around materialism and greed. It is phony, selfish, and a fantasy land. The American Dream has nothing to do with love or God.

Now let's get on to my expectation of a wife: one word - Barbie!!! I wanted a woman who looked like Barbie and took care of a house like June Cleaver from *Leave it to Beaver*. Looking back, I can clearly see the phony character I had created in my mind. I wanted someone who did not even exist.

Everything previously mentioned is all materialism. To clarify, I don't believe there is anything wrong with having toys or material objects. However, when they become your God there is a problem. When they are idols you worship there is a problem. **Exodus 20:1-3** (NKJV) clearly states, "And God spoke all these words saying, "I am the Lord your God who brought you out of the land of Egypt, out of the house of bondage. You shall have no other gods before me." I obviously had a serious problem.

I also envisioned myself as a tycoon of a company. One of those bosses who had a secretary so he didn't have to talk to the people who worked for him. Someone who greedily cut bonuses short so he could take a bigger bonus, a man who would do anything to get to the top.

You have not heard me mention love yet, have you? What was love? Why did I need love? The people on TV did not really love each other, they were just acting. I watched my parents get divorced when I was six years old, so I definitely had false ideas of what a marriage was to be like. I wanted what I saw on television: the phoniness, the acting, "the good life" that didn't take any work. Fortunately I found out later that this was not reality.

As I grew, I had no idea what career path would get me this American dream. One major issue I had growing up was that I despised school. I was an outcast and not in with the cool crowd. This did quite a bit of damage to me in high school. I skipped class most of the time and learned to do things on my terms and not the terms of the authority body, meaning the school administration. The teachers and principals could never understand why I was doing stupid things. They kept telling me I was too smart to be in this kind of trouble. To be quite honest with you I just didn't care. I had no desire to be there or learn anything. I was in a major period of rebellion in my life. I just wanted to do it my way. Well that's OK if you're not living under the roof of your parents. For some reason, I thought I was going to just strike it rich and not have to deal with finding a career. That was really not so. So how was I going to attain this American dream without the education I needed? I struggled through high school and through most of my college years. As you find out later, I learned that there was no such thing as a free lunch, nor did I want it to be given to me.

The American Dream

Although I struggled, I did survive high school and I distinctly remember my graduation day. My dad flew in from California to witness my graduation so I decided to stay in the hotel with him for a couple of days. It was one of the many seedy hotels in my city - one that attracted prostitutes and drug dealers. On the day of my graduation, my dad spoke the following words over me that took me years to recuperate from hearing, "Son, forget about the American dream, and go work at the post office. You won't ever amount to anything greater in life then a postman, and at least you will have a pension after 30 years." These fatalistic words of discouragement were a crushing blow to me. They are words that stuck with me for most of my life. Have you ever had someone abuse you with their words? Have you ever had someone close to you, like your father, speak words of death over you? It's such an awful feeling. Here is a man who is my father who is supposed to support me, help me, encourage me, and teach me about life. Dictionary.com defines a Father as the following: a man who exercises paternal care over other persons; paternal protector or provider: *a father to the poor.*

Something was missing in my relationship with my dad. Out of fairness to him, he had no way of knowing how to be a parent to me. And I have told him many times that I have forgiven him for his actions and words and for the fact that he didn't know how to help and guide me. My father had a horrible example to learn from. My grandfather was a man of many negative words and was raised in Russia. He was the true definition of the term, "Russian Bear." I do need to admit that my father's words pushed and motivated me for quite a while to keep chasing the American dream.

It's only by the grace of God that I managed to graduate college with a 3.71 GPA in my major. It wasn't your typical picture of school. It took me seven years to complete. Let me share with you some of the reasons it took me so long. I flunked out of the first Community College I attended. I then found a loophole that allowed me to transfer to another Community College. I then lost the records of my flunking out so they accepted me as a new student.

College was a whole different experience for me. It was so nice. They did not take roll in the class, and I could skip class whenever I wanted. I remember them telling me I should be studying, but I wanted nothing to do with it. I wanted to party. I was out of the house and I wanted to drink alcohol, smoke pot, and have sex. By now I was really out of my comfort zone and I decided that eating would become a sport for me as well. I moved from Orlando to Tallahassee, which is big city to small town. I was so uncomfortable there and did not have any way to cope with the change I was experiencing. I wanted to be drunk every night of the week, but that was not in my budget. I had to find a way to do this without wrecking my finances. I found Old English 800! Yes! I started to drink what some refer to as 40's, but in Florida they are sold in 32 oz better known as A Quart or The Q. I use to leave the bottle in a brown paper bag like I saw the gangsters do in the movies. Yep - back to following the movies again. You will notice that living vicariously through the movies was a common theme in my life. So every day I would purchase 2 bottles of "Old E" as we called it. It was .79 cents per bottle and I was now able to get drunk for $1.58 per day. WOW...how messed up was that?

    I finally had a serious girlfriend as well, but my big issue with her was that she would not have sex with me. You must understand I was a 21 year old walking hormone with a lust addiction. The sex I experienced in my teenage years was mostly one night stands, but now I wanted sex with a girlfriend. I wanted sex like the movies or soap operas, morning, afternoon, evening, and middle of the night. This girlfriend was not a great influence on me, although she was the one who got me to stop drinking the Old E. Shortly after that, I dumped her and moved back to one night stands so that women were not able to know me.

    Somehow with all this going on I managed to graduate with my AA degree from Tallahassee Community College. I still remember one of my professors, who actually stood up and cheered for me as I received my A.A. Degree. He and my mom were the only people who cheered for me.

I decided to transfer again to Florida Atlantic University this time. I was taking classes in Sociology and then switched my major to Criminal Justice. I took classes in Sociology to meet women! I had always been told I had ADHD, and so I had requested help from tutors and note-takers for my classes. In one of my Criminal Justice classes, the professor asked in front of the class for someone to take notes for a slow person in class. He was supposed to ask the note taker to come and talk to him after class and then privately connect us. When someone volunteered the professor identified me as the slow person and told me to talk to the note-taker after class. I went to file a report against the professor and was told it was a waste of time because he was tenured. I decided to rebel and dropped out of college before they kicked me out because of my grades. The only person this hurt was me.

I was working full time at this point and seeing a therapist because I was a mess. She told me about a school called The Union Institute where she got her Doctorate in Miami. I explained to her that I was a horrible student and had a bad track record with school. She made me promise that I would call them and go have an interview and listen to them about the programs they had. So I did!

The American Dream

As I followed her suggestion, I met a man named Dr. Mike. He explained their program was accredited and the majority of the students worked full time and came one night a week for the first semester and then did the classes via correspondence with their professors after that. He looked at all my transcripts and told me I could get a Bachelors degree in Business Administration in three semesters. He said I should have graduated by that point because of all the credits I had. He told me he believed in me and that he knew this was the correct program for me. He told me to try it and give it a chance. I took five classes per semester for the next three semesters and finally graduated with a 3.71 in Business Administration. What a miracle!

The Fantasy of the American dream was so appealing to me. I lived my life in a fantasy land. I lived vicariously through TV personalities and characters on sit-coms. Anytime one of them would go to prison or do something unlawful I would be crushed. I distinctly remember that every time one of them fell, I chopped them to the ground and murdered them with my words after their fall. I talked about how stupid they were and how dumb they could be to have so much and throw it all away in drugs and crime.

I was quite the hypocrite. My drug and alcohol abuse started in my high school years and with a brief lapse of about one year, continued into my college years and my early twenties. I wanted to party like the rock stars I watched on TV. This took me into a very seedy period of my life.

I finally started my career in sales and got to find out some harsh realities. The reality was my first full time sales job paid a base salary of $24,000 per year plus $2,500 of commission if I could sell enough to get it. The days and nights were long and I adopted the role of a traveling salesman. Some of you think the road is a great place, but for me, it was a place where I had to make life decisions between good and evil.

You have now seen a picture of where my heart was. In the next chapter I will show you more about who I was. I will share some of my **deepest** emotions and darkest times with you. You will also see how much life was all about me, myself, and the devil. The man I am today is only possible because of our Lord and Savior Jesus Christ! Jesus got a hold of me, and I know He can do the same for you!

2 - Me, Myself, and the Devil!

Have you ever wondered what your purpose was? Well that's what I experienced for most of my life. I often woke up wondering what I would choose to do each day. I woke up most days focusing on me, myself, and the devil. I would certainly learn what it meant to be thrust into the fire of Hell.

We are taught to be able to support ourselves in this world and be independent. I think back to a statement a great woman of God spoke. She said, "My priority as a parent should be to gradually transfer my child's dependence from me to where they fully rely on God." You heard nothing in this statement about being independent from and away from God. Why does society teach us to do this? I think this goes back to the American dream, which is about me, myself and I. The Bible tells us in **Philippians 4:13** (NKJV) "I can do all things through Christ who strengthens me." Isn't it funny how we so often find ourselves seeking strength from everything else but Christ.

Me, Myself, and the Devil!

I was never taught anything about relying on God. I grew up in a Jewish home, so there was no talk about Jesus Christ in my home. I knew to rely on my parents and at some point I would have to rely on myself. So that's what I eventually did. After I graduated college, I relied on myself. During the time I was in college I picked up many bad habits and spent many years playing around with drugs and alcohol. I was stuck. I would try many different careers and dream many different dreams, all trying to find myself. I was so lonely and found myself in some very dark places.

I ended up doing things that I never thought I would do. I ended up serving someone I did not even believe existed. I remember having a conversation with my friend, we'll call him "Bob," one day when we were working. I was sharing with him about the partying I did the night before. Now understand I was Bob's boss at the time. Also understand that Bob was a Christian and I was not. I continued to share with him about how much I drank and how good the strippers looked, and how much I gambled the night before. He had to be bleeding on the inside knowing how much I needed Jesus. As I continued to share with him, he let me know that I was living my life for the devil. At that time I told him there was no such thing as the devil or heaven and hell. If you ever try to convince yourself there is no such thing as the devil, then I can guarantee you that the devil has you in his grips and you are serving the devil and none other than him.

Amazingly Bob stepped back and started to pray quietly for me. I asked him why he was praying for me. He told me he was praying for my soul. He told me that even though I did not believe in Jesus that Jesus still knew everything I was doing and that He still loved me in spite of it all. I asked him how he knew that and he told me that the Bible told him this. I pretty much laughed at him and told him that the Bible was not relevant for living today.

I hope you're getting the picture of how far gone I was. Bob told me that he and his family prayed every night for me. I thought, "Wow, this dude is really a Jesus Freak." I thanked him for caring so much for me and told him I would be just fine. At that point I am sure he knew I was the crazy one and not him!

In my early 20's there was no God in my life at all. I had, however, discovered the Occult. I was visiting psychics and tarot card readers regularly. I even got a job at a metaphysical book store because, as I told you before, I was trying to find myself. I immersed myself in this way of life. I spent most of my days trying to be close to who I thought was God. Little did I know I was nestling up to demons and demonic forces. I had opened myself up to everything that was not God yet looked like God. I was truly deceived by what I thought was the way to a happy life. It wasn't until years later that I developed a full understanding of the evil I had opened my heart up to.

John 10:10 (NKJV) says, "The thief does not come except to steal, and to kill, and to destroy. I have come that they may have life, and that they may have it more abundantly."

I can assure you that the "thief" was out to destroy my life.

People sometimes wonder how to know if something is God or the devil. Well, you can definitely reference this scripture. I opened my heart up to a world that was filled with darkness, yet I expected light to come out of this. I had been led there by someone who believed the same lies that I started to believe. I noticed I tried to draw many people into this world, and most knew what it was about. It was about sorcery, darkness, and hidden agendas. It had nothing to do with grace, mercy, and love. It had nothing to do with these things because they are of Jesus. I used to ask all the metaphysical people if they believed in Jesus, and none of them could give me a straight answer. Many of the people I hung around with believed in multiple gods. They used to pray to the spirits, and I am not talking about the Holy Spirit! They would also pray to Buddha or Hindu gods such as Vishnu or Shiva. Some even prayed to gods or idols they had simply made up themselves.

I was so centered on myself at this time of my life that I did not know where to turn. I was just about to get married for the first time in my life and did not even know who I was. I was still trying to finish college while I worked full time. I was living in Southeast Florida, and my girlfriend who would later become my wife, was living in Orlando. I finally moved back to Orlando and faced a huge storm that I had been avoiding for the previous 5 years. I was still running from people and situations in Orlando that I had left unresolved. I was trying to start a new period of my life, yet was still very much living the previous period of my life. I still had no knowledge of Jesus and no desire to have a personal relationship with him. There is a verse of scripture that really hammers this home:

Matthew 9:17 (NKJV)

> 17 Nor do they put new wine into old wineskins, or else the wineskins break, the wine is spilled, and the wineskins are ruined. But they put new wine into new wineskins, and both are preserved."

I had physically tried to put new wine into the old wine skins.

My life was a mess. My friends did not know me, I did not know who I was, my soon to be wife really did not know me. Nothing was going my way. So at this point I decided to take a job in sales in addition to school. I failed miserably in this job. I was selling cell phones to offices door to door. What a tough way to learn about sales! I went on after that to take two other small jobs out of sales for a while, so I could lick my wounds and my bruised ego.

After a brief period away from sales I went back into it and started to travel for work. The territory I covered required me to be on the road most of the time. Many people seem to have this opinion that work travel is glamorous. I am here to tell you...it's not! I spent my nights in seedy motels. I had a budget of $55.00 per night and stayed mostly in motels that had prostitution and drug abuse.

Life on the road was hard. I worked ten hours a day then drove 200 miles to the next stop; and after all that I stayed in terrible motels that were loud and places I could never get a good night of sleep. They were not clean or comfortable. It was a tough life. On top of the low motel per diem, we had a food budget of $25.00 per day. This was not a lot and I ate fast food most of the time.

I hated this job because my boss used to cuss us out every Friday morning on the conference call we had. We could never do anything right in his eyes. As I was married by now, I did not get to see my wife from Monday-Friday each week as I left Monday morning and came home Friday afternoon.

This was a hard way to live but would become a way of life for me for many years to come. Mostly what I did in the evening on the road was drink alcohol. I was so lonely at this time and felt completely unlovable. As I would have good weeks where I sold many widgets, I would take the extra money and go to the topless bars with my money to gain acceptance. Most of the women I hung out with there were drug addicts and alcoholics and would agree with whatever I said just to take my money.

During this time of my life, one of the dearest people in the world to me, Nana Sadie, was at the end of her life. She was the best grandma a kid could have. She loved me so much. She was always there for me and always stood behind me in whatever I was doing. She used to cook such great Jewish food for me and blessed me with her cooking. She was in a nursing home and had suffered some gangrene and was fighting cirrhosis of the liver. I use to visit her every Thursday or Friday when I was on my way back into town from my business trips. I would then come on the weekend as well. The nursing home had a Shi Tzu Dog named Molly who my Nana loved very much. She was always a dog lover and I used to take Molly out of her pen and bring her into my Nana's bed so she could play with her. It was very hard for me to watch my Nana die slowly over a three month period. She finally passed while I was in California for Labor Day weekend in 2001. I kept wondering why she had to go and often return myself to one particular scripture which helps me understand the way God looks at death.

Me, Myself, and the Devil!

Isaiah 57:1-2 (NLT) 57 Good people pass away; the Godly often die before their time. But no one seems to care or wonder why. No one seems to understand that God is protecting them from the evil to come. 2 For those who follow Godly paths will rest in peace when they die.

My Nana died just days before September 11, 2001 and the attacks on New York City and Washington DC. At that point in her life, it would have devastated my Nana to have lived through these events. God knew this and took her home before these events happened. It was such a sad time in my life. I cried and cried because I missed her so much. She truly loved me unconditionally. We shared such good times throughout my childhood. I remember when she used to babysit me when my mom went out. We had such great times together and she use to always let me stay up later then I was supposed to. The greatest memory I have of her is how much she loved to serve me and cook for me. She would iron clothes for me as I got older and did anything she could to bless and serve me. She was very special in my life and her death was a devastating blow to me.

At this time I was trying to make my marriage work amidst all my travel, internal confusion, and lack of self-esteem. I came to believe that I had nothing to offer my wife. This belief prevented me from ever being the husband I was called to be. I allowed the road to pollute me. I allowed the things of the devil to be constants in my life. I allowed the forces of darkness to live inside of me. I was at what I thought was the bottom, but as I would find out, I had much further down to go.

After my Nana's death there was an explosion of turmoil in my life. My wife and I was trying to move into a new house, and my father had to have quadruple bypass heart surgery and ended up in a coma for three months. I felt so alone - like my whole world had caved in on me and that I had nowhere to turn. I really started to drink heavily at this time to escape the wreckage that was my life.

Work at this time was also very stressful, and to make matters worse, I had to visit my Dad often at the hospital. It was excruciating for me to watch him living in a coma. Although my Dad had not been the epitome of a perfect father, I still loved him dearly. Each week I met with the doctors and talked with them about his progress. Often times they told me to just turn the life support off and let him die. One doctor would not let me do that. He kept telling me that my dad would make full recovery, and I desperately wanted to believe him so I kept my Dad hooked up to the life support until one day he finally came out of the coma and back to life. He wasn't able to talk because he had a tracheotomy and had a tube stuck in his throat. He was able to look at me and acknowledge me. I remember the day we put the valve in the trach so he could speak.

Me, Myself, and the Devil!

The first words out of his mouth were four letter words. He wanted to know what happened. He told me he thought he died. He wanted to know what the future looked like, and I expressed that it would be a hard road but that he would lead a normal life again.

My self-worth at this time was in material things. I thought the house my wife and I were building was the answer to all my problems. It was in a new gated community and was supposed to make me happy, but I was not. At this point the breakdown of my marriage started to take place. When a person is on the road as much as I was their spouse often begins to get comfortable with sleeping alone. When I came home each week it was hard for her to get adjusted to having me sleep in the bed next to her, especially with the loud snoring I was doing! We ended up sleeping in separate beds. I would caution couples, that if you ever start to sleep in separate beds, this is a cause to be concerned and you should seek some help from a pastor or counselor. We spent five months in this house together before we could not take it anymore and decided to separate and eventually divorce. We had not even been married for two years when we divorced.

I was a complete mess. I had dealt with some very traumatic situations but not in a way that was healthy. Later in my life I would end up dealing with all of these situations and gaining healing for them. I am ready to guide you into the next chapter of my life. This was my climb up the corporate ladder.

3 - Climbing the Corporate Ladder

After my divorce, I focused my attention on my career and climbing the corporate ladder. I was with a good company who saw a lot of potential in me. I was covering all of Florida for them as a Sales Rep selling lawn and garden equipment. I had been with the company a little over a year, and things seemed to be working well. The only issue was that I was traveling four to five nights every week. I left town on Mondays and came home on Fridays. Things seemed to be stable, and I started to date my wife, Alice. She was refreshing to have in my life and we started to fall in love. It was amazing that she put up with my travel. Once again I was *Thrust into the Fire.*

One day as I was driving through Florida I received a phone call from my boss indicating that I was being promoted me to Assistant Sales Manager for my region. They explained that I would need to hire four people to cover my territory, and I would train them and manage them. As this happened, there was a big project that was dropped in my lap to execute. So in the middle of hiring and training I had two teams of people to manage to ensure the project got done the way we wanted it done. My team executed well and we ended up getting a very large contract to handle. This meant that I would need to hire 12 more employees, and I was now promoted to Regional Sales Manager. I now had a total of 15 employees and an Assistant Sales Manager. Over the next couple years we would have a great run of sales and customer service.

    One of the low points while I worked for this company was a young man who I will call "Chris." I first met him when he was referred to our company by his mom. He was in his early 20's and was eager to work. We hired him after he spent a day working with me. I knew Chris liked to party like I did but did not know when we hired him how much he liked to party. Chris worked hard for a while until he felt that he had earned the right to goof off a bit. I started to hear some things from my office about his expense reports and the fact that he submitted condom receipts for reimbursement when he was on the road. I chose to look the other way as Chris was a good employee most of the time. One day I was at a customer's store and they informed me they had not seen Chris for a while; however, I had seen this very person's signature on many of his weekly reports over the last three months. This led to the discovery that he had been forging her name. I pulled some other reports and found that he had been forging signatures on all reports. I decided to do further background by calling another employee. I came to learn that "Chris" was not the good employee that I thought he was. He had been snorting cocaine on his breaks during the day and was stoned or hung over all the time. I did what I needed to do which was to terminate Chris. It was very hard for me to do as I looked at Chris as a little brother. One week after I terminated him he called me and apologized. He told me he had problems and said he was sorry for what happened. I told him I forgave him and wished him the best. Three weeks after that phone call, I received a call on a Friday morning from his girlfriend informing me he had died. I was numb when I heard this. It was the first time I had lost an employee or former employee. I started to examine my own life and saw how deep I was thrust into the fire of hell, but I did not want to change.

Not long after this, the company I worked for ended up having a contest to find the best sales region in the country. There were 20 regions and we competed against each other for ten months The areas we competed against each other were: employee retention, productivity, efficiency, amount of work completed, accuracy of work completed, and expenditure management. My region won unanimously. Each of my employees received a small bonus, and I received a $5000.00 bonus. I was presented the award at the national managers meeting. It was an exciting time, until I was brought into a private meeting and confronted about a situation that had taken place. About two months previous to the meeting, the owner's son called me at 11:30 one evening and asked me to do some work which kept me up until 4:00 a.m. Now at this time I was working 16 hours a day, five days a week. After that phone call I had complained to the owner about his son calling me so late. The owner and his son had a rocky relationship and the owner decided to tell his son what I said, even though he told me it would stay between us. The owner's son ripped me up in a meeting after he had just given me a big award. He told me that I had no right to complain and that he would make my life a living hell. Now understand at this time I was not a Christian and this man was a Christian and threatening to make my life a living hell. He told me that there was a new level of management being opened up and I was passed over for this promotion by one of the other guys who they felt was a better fit for the position and who never questioned what they asked him to do. I was devastated. I should have come home from this trip excited, but instead came home very upset.

  I went back to work and continued to push on. My new boss was terrible and gave me a hard time every chance he got. Nothing I did was good enough. Finally the straw that broke the camel's back was the reward check that came. The check was supposed to have taxes paid by the company and it did not. Also, the owner's son did not sign the check. When I questioned them about the check, they told me I had to pay my own taxes. I found the email where I had been told that the company would pay the taxes and they told me they never wrote it. About four weeks later I received a check for $3,800.00 instead of $5,000.00. This was it for me. I emailed my resignation to the company.

About two days later the owner called me and asked me why I was leaving. I told him it was time for me to move on. He told me the resignation letter hit his desk with a thud and that it was completely unexpected. I told him due to the current situation and being passed over for the promotion and the issue with his son, it was time for me to leave. He told me he was not going to try and keep me. I was even more upset now. I spent five years of my life building their business and they did not even want to try and work something out to keep me. It showed me where I stood with the company. Right before I left I hired a guy to work in Waycross, GA. He was 60 years old and excited about being able to work again as he had been laid off for two years. We sent him to Jacksonville, FL for training. The first two days he did great, and then Tuesday night had a stroke and died in his hotel room. This was really hard for me to deal with, but I went out to party to numb the emotions. Losing two employees was really hard, but this would not be the last time I lost someone. I

Climbing the Corporate Ladder

have always cared for my employees as if they are family. It was always hard to receive those phone calls.

Looking back, I clearly see that I left this job due to pride and because I felt disrespected. I felt they were treating me wrongly, and that I was too good to be talked to like this. By leaving this job I put my family in a bad place financially. I was now married to Alice, and I put her in a situation where she did not feel secure. She was out of work at this time on short term disability, and so we now had no income coming in. I decided to go back to driving Lincoln Town cars for a chauffeur service. I had worked there previously and thought I could make good money there again. When I worked there previously I made $1,200.00 per week. This time I struggled to make $600.00 per week. It was a very rough time in my life. We had not cut our spending at this time, and were racking up credit card bills. To help pay off some of the credit cards, we went ahead and took a second mortgage out on the house to help pay our debts off. We really were not paying any of the debt down, and we were robbing from Peter to pay Paul. I will tell you that this is not a good practice. We really need to seek the Word of God on being good stewards of our finances.

> **Philippians 4:19** (NKJV) says, "And my God shall supply all your need according to His riches in glory by Christ Jesus."

Alice and I did not understand anything about stewardship of our finances. We always figured we could run the bills up because I would get a good job and we would be able to pay the bills off. Well at this point that had not happened. I was so miserable driving for a living and was just waiting for a different job opportunity. At that time a former boss of mine called me and said he was with a new company and they were hiring. He gave me the name of the divisional sales manager and I called him and we hit it off. This company had just received 100 product lines in the lumber department and I was now their regional sales manager for Florida. This company loved how I handled things and this was a good partnership for both of us. I went back to working 80-90 hours per week again and hired some of my old crew from the last company.

I had a good crew working for me here at this company, but it did not compare to my crew at the previous company. These guys were different and I had some rookies I needed to change. Most of them were good guys, but I did have some others I had issues with. One of the guys I really liked turned out to have a problem with sexual harassment. He ended up getting terminated and in serious legal trouble because of his behavior.

One of my highlights with this company was a guy I'll call "Mike" that I had hired with the previous company that I brought over to work with me. I hired him as my Assistant Sales Manager and told him one day I would leave and my job would be his. He was a seasoned veteran in our industry and in his 40's. He had lived a rough life and was very happy now and finally felt successful. We traveled the road together and he helped me so much. It was a huge blessing to have him on board and working hand in hand with me. I truly took him under my wing and taught him everything he needed to know. I had been with the company about eight months when I started to feel it was time to go do something else. I prepped Mike more and more and told him he was on a two week crash course to get ready to take over. I had decided to partner in business with my best friend of 25 years. We had started with me working part time on the side, and got ready for me to come aboard full time. On a Friday we decided that I would make my announcement at work that Monday and leave the company to go out into my new venture. I called Mike and told him about the news and said I would resign Monday morning and that I would set him up to be promoted and take over for me. He was all excited and his family was happy as well. On Sunday night before he was to be promoted, he finished dinner and had a heart attack and died in his chair on his back porch. His wife called me immediately after and I decided to delay my decision. I was crushed, angry, frustrated, and just could not comprehend what happened.

In the coming days I went through a time where I blamed myself for Mike's passing. I felt maybe I pushed him too hard, and that I shoved him toward something he did not want. Actually, none of this was true, and he died because of a lifestyle of abusing his body with harmful things. I think of Mike often today because he was such a special person to me in my life, and I was so happy to see his life turning around. I spoke at his funeral, and had a hard time holding back tears.

I waited about three weeks after the funeral and then turned in my resignation. I went to work with my best friend and partnered in his IT Services Company. At this time I was trying to keep friendships with previous bosses and employees. My old boss was so angry at me because he felt that I left a mess when I left. He accused me of many things and most of all was not training my employees well enough. Unfortunately this was not the truth. The truth was the day I quit the guys stopped working hard and some even working at all, because I left. They were loyal to me and worked hard for me and knew how much I cared for them, but they did not feel the same way about the company and did not show the company the same love they showed me. After about six months, my old boss called me and made peace with me. It was good to make up and we would never talk again after this.

I was now in what I thought would be my dream job and the company I would build into a force to be reckoned with in the Orlando area. I was working 7 a.m. to 10 p.m. five days a week now and doing everything I could to make this business run. We increased sales by 300 % in the first two years I was there. We hired more staff and even hired an office manager so I could assume the role of the Vice President of Operations. We were starting to make some good money for the company, but we had spent a lot to get there. Also at this time we realized we were overpaying our employees. My business partner and I were having a lot of trouble getting along as well. The fighting caused our company to go through tremendous problems and we were not firing on all cylinders. It was time for me think about making some changes.

    My identity was completely wrapped up in my work. My wife was very frustrated with me because I was not paying any attention to her, and our marriage was suffering. We started to talk about divorce. We both thought we wanted out. As we talked about this, we realized that we did not like each other but were still in love with each other. We went on a cruise for our vacation and decided to start trying to get to know each other again. This was a very dark time in my life. My wife did not like me, my business partner did not like me, my family did not like me, and I was just plain old miserable. I thought that climbing the corporate ladder would make me happy. I didn't know where to turn for my happiness. At this time I had been hearing what I thought to be the Lord Jesus speak to me each week and tell me to go to a church and hear the Word of God. Well I just could not get the strength up to do this. Every Sunday I tried to go but would not get out of bed. I had started watching TBN and other Christian stations religiously. Even with as many things as I heard on these stations, I still could not get the strength up to go.

My life was complete misery. I had chased the American dream and had tried everything to make myself happy, but nothing had worked. I labored so hard but for the past 32 years I could not put anything together to make me happy. As you will learn in the next chapter I was looking in the wrong places. This story is about to get really good. Keep reading and find out what happens to me that changes my life forever. What is about to take place is the most significant event in my life. It changed me and just reading about it will change you too. Get on the train as we go to the next period of my life and find out how I was thrust into the fire of God!

4 - Jesus? Are You For Real?

In October 2006, my wife and I continued to struggle in our marriage. Things had progressively gotten worse over the past years. As you can probably tell by now my focus was not on my wife but was on my career and seeking the American dream. I remember how angry I was at my wife for not catering to my every need. I was so selfish and it was all about what she could do to please me, and not what I could do to be a better husband. Finally we had a big argument and I thought my marriage was over. At this time work was pretty bad and I was fighting with my business partner often. Then I would come home to an angry wife. My wife and I decided that we should take a cruise together in December of 2006. We took a week long cruise and realized that we no longer liked each other. There was one good spot though is that we both knew we were in love with each other. We spent a week together focused on each other. This helped us get closer to each other then we had been in a long time.

When we got off the cruise ship we were back to reality, and I was trying really hard to love her. It's really hard to love someone when you hate your own life and who you have become. I decided to start going to a therapist again for counseling. I had been to therapists most of my life since the time of my parent's divorce which was when I was six.

    The reason I went to see the therapist is because I was one step away from a nervous breakdown. I remember sitting in my office at work closing my door because I just could not deal with anything else anymore. I had never felt that way in my life before, but things had gotten so out of hand that all I could do was cry and drink alcohol. I went to see the therapist and the first session went really well. He basically confirmed for me that I did not know who I was, who I wanted to be, or who God had called me to be. My whole existence and self-worth came from work, which at the time was at an all-time low. We were having trouble meeting payroll and business had slowed to a crawl. It was panic time at work. I left the therapist office knowing I needed to go see him a couple of times per week to help me through this turbulence. I did ask the therapist about Jesus because I knew he was a Christian. He told me that Jesus was real and encouraged me to seek what He had for me. I saw the therapist on a Thursday and went to church on Sunday morning January 7, 2007.

    As I entered the church I was the most scared I had ever been. It was nothing like I imagined. The music was contemporary, the pastor was cool and told me to call him by his first name, and the people were friendly. I put some good clothes on so they would not know what a mess I was. So many times in life we cover our wounds with clothes and makeup so that people do not know what they are. I can tell you that these people knew who I was and how bad I was hurting. They were very nice and welcomed me. The church was seven minutes from my house which made it even more enticing to attend. The service lasted about one hour and fifteen minutes, and I was relieved when it was over. One of the most important things that the pastor preached that day was Romans 5:8.

> **Romans 5:8** (NKJV) "But God demonstrates His own love toward us, in that while we were still sinners, Christ died for us."

Wow - did I need to hear that! Because I did not grow up in the church or with Christianity, I thought I had to be perfect to come to Christ. I had no clue that He loves us while we were still sinners. When I heard that the lights and bells went off. It was like I just hit the lottery. I saw flashing lights before my eyes and buzzers ringing. A miracle had happened. I was waiting for the end of the service to come and answer the altar call. When we got to the end and there was no altar call, I knew what needed to take place later that day. I thanked the pastor and assured him I would be back. I went home and dropped to my knees and cried out for Jesus to enter my life and told him I would make him my Lord and Savior! I remember I was on my knees on the rug and sat there weeping for about three hours as my wife was not home. I was now thrust into the fire of God!

At this time I still did not know much about being a Christian. I just knew things needed to change. I told the Lord how bad I needed him and how much I needed him to change things. I could not stop weeping. I finally realized that Jesus was real! The next week I went to church and started to talk to my new friend. I'll call him "Fred." He was very wise and encouraging. He gave me his number and told me to call him if I needed to talk. I did call him and we started a friendship. He was very instrumental in helping me through my early walk. He had scripture in his heart and had an awesome relationship with the Lord. I looked to him to guide me as I in my new walk with the Lord. He invited me to a small group, and I started to come. It was really cool to sit in someone's house and talk about the real truth about what had happened that week in our lives. It was also awesome to hear testimonies from people about what God had done in their lives the week before.

One day I remember Fred asking me if I was reading the Word of God. I told him that was for the pastor to read and asked him why I should read it. He started to educate me about reading the Bible daily. I remember telling him how I did not like to read, and him telling me that to seek to be closer with God, I needed to know what His word says. I started to read the Word of God and within a week of reading it things began to happen.

As you might imagine, my wife thought I had gone completely crazy. When I invited her to church she did not want to go. Eventually God would bring us together and I would lead her to the Lord. I made a decision to leave the company of which I was a co-owner and go back to corporate America. This decision meant more to my wife than I even realized. She was exceedingly happy when I called her and told her I would be leaving. I had only been saved three weeks at this time, so this was a huge step for me. I remember seeking council from my friend, Fred, to make sure I was hearing from the Lord and following the path He called me to. As it would turn out this would be one of the best decisions I made in my life. Also, this decision would show my wife that there was a God because she had been praying that I would leave the company and go back to a corporate job. I want to be clear that things in my life were not perfect. Anyone who tells you when you come to know Jesus that your life is going to be perfect is lying to you. What I can tell you is that my worst and toughest days with Jesus are still 100 times better than my best days without Jesus.

Jesus? Are You For Real?

My marriage was still struggling, but I learned about praying for my wife. I also learned that reading the Bible taught me how to be a better husband. I know my wife was thinking, "What happened to my husband?" She was very aware that I was going through a major change, and she was having a hard time figuring out what happened to me. After about three months my wife started to come to church with me. She was having a rough time in her life but saw something so drastic and radical taking place in me that she wanted what was happening to me. I could not explain it. All the things I had heard about Jesus: the signs, miracles, and wonders, were starting to take place.

I remember going for a job interview with a company and in the interview they told me that the position paid a lot less than what I was currently making. I prayed and asked the Lord to make the offer 10,000 dollars higher if He wanted me to take that job. The guy was supposed to call me back within one week and let me know if I was going to get the job or not. I did not hear from him for four weeks. While I was making a presentation for my company, the man left me a voicemail on my phone and said to call him. I called him back and he asked me if I was ready for a new career, and of course I said yes. He told me the offer was 10,000 dollars higher than we originally talked about. My prayer had been answered and this was a sign it was time to go. I put my final notice in and made my preparations to leave the company and move into the role of a silent partner. Two years later I gave my ownership back to my business partner without any compensation for it. It was the right thing to do, and it was what God instructed me to do.

Now I know you're thinking that it sounds like things were getting better, but in all actuality they would get much more challenging. This new job I started required me to spend five weeks of training in Wisconsin. It required that I fly to Madison for two weeks then come home for two days, then to the field for one week, then home for two days, and back to Madison for two more weeks. This was not the time of my life to be doing this, but I knew that God wanted me to take this job. I met a man I'll call "Nick" in training the first day. He had been in the HVAC industry for 30 years and I had been in it for one day. Nick and I instantly bonded and God knew I needed him. He was a spirit-filled Episcopal. I had no clue what that meant, but later in my journey I would meet another one and understand things a little better.

This new job was very technical and scientific, both of which I was not. I was a Salesman, a Sales Manager, a VP of Operations, a District Manager, not a technical salesman of HVAC products. See this was God killing Brad and building a new man in his image and not my image. I remember telling Nick I wanted to quit every day of the week we were together. He told me with my personality and sales ability that I would do great. He promised me he would teach me the technical side of things and help me if I stayed on board. So I realized God had sent Nick to me, and I focused on learning what I needed so I could be a great dehumidifier salesman.

As I had started to get involved in my church, I was seeking fellowship with other Christian men. About this time, Fred decided to start up a Bible study group at 6 a.m. each week. That meant I would need to get up around 4:30 am. I do not like being up before 7 a.m. and now I was being asked to be up at 4:30 am! By now I knew I had gone nuts, and my wife was really confused. I did not miss a week for a long time. This group meant so much to me. There were usually four to six of us who met regularly. What took place in this group was amazing. We called the group "Iron Men." I'm reminded of **Proverbs 27:17** (NKJV) "As iron sharpens iron, so a man sharpens the countenance of his friend."

This was a fitting name, as our conversations strengthened each other, our struggles made us wise, and our triumphs lifted each other up. God poured out His spirit on this group and it was exactly what I needed as a new believer. The transformation that had taken place in my life was absolutely incredible. I went from listening to "We're not Gonna Take It" by Twisted Sister, to "Awesome God" by Rich Mullins. I just wanted to get to know Jesus better.

Jesus? Are You For Real?

One of the best things happened next. My wife got saved! Now this did not happen in the easiest way. I had been on a business trip and had come home to a very depressed wife. She had been diagnosed bi-polar earlier in her life and had struggled ever since with this illness. I came home from the trip on Friday afternoon and took her out to dinner. She had been sleeping 18 hours a day at this point. I had to make a decision what to do. On Saturday morning I called her therapist and her psychiatrist and the three of us made a decision for me to put her in the hospital. This was the hardest thing I ever had to do in my life, but knew I needed to do it. My wife agreed to go because she knew she needed help. I knew she was not happy with me at the time, but she would thank me later for saving her life. She was hospitalized for six days and came out a new woman. I will never forget visiting her each day at the hospital after work and watching my wife get healthy. It was a miracle only God could have done. When she came out of the hospital she came to church with me and gave her life to the Lord and was baptized in water the week after. This moved me and really showed me who God was. I could not believe the change that happened in my wife. Her medications were regulated and she was feeling great. Over the next year she lost over 100 pounds. The coolest thing is that God started to heal her heart toward our marriage, and for the first time we started to walk together as husband and wife.

> **Ephesians 5:22-25** (NKJV)
> 22Wives, submit to your own husbands, as to the Lord. 23 For the husband is head of the wife, as also Christ is head of the church; and He is the Savior of the body. 24 Therefore, just as the church is subject to Christ, so let the wives be to their own husbands in everything.25 Husbands, love your wives, just as Christ also loved the church and gave Himself for her.

I was starting to finally understand the role Christ had called me to as a husband. As I walked through this I watched my marriage shift and our love for one another grow. I watched my wife allow me to lead for the first time in our marriage. I once asked her why, and she told me she finally trusted me in the direction that I was leading her. She had seen God change me so miraculously there was nothing she could do but come along. I am praying at this point that you will continue to come along with me as I share the rest of this journey with you.

5 - The Calling

A year and a half after receiving Christ, I found myself with an insatiable hunger for God. I was still attending the same church I got saved in and the assistant pastor really reached out to me. He helped me get focused on serving the Lord and seeking my call. I will call what happens next the pre-call.

I had started to serve in the youth ministry of the church and found it very rewarding. I did not know how to relate to the youth but was doing the best I could, and I believe they could tell where my heart was. The assistant pastor kept telling me I was called to be a youth pastor. I just did not feel that was my call. Remember I did not know much about how churches operate and so I did not know that many times pastors are youth pastors before they become senior pastors. I was thankful that someone in a position of authority in the church recognized that God was calling me to ministry.

My problem was that I did not feel like youth pastor material or ministry material at all. I was still carrying around emotional baggage from my past life, but I was about to get a big surprise. The pastor of the church was involved in an activity that would later cause him to leave the church. I was crushed. I loved this man and realized that my faith was in him sometimes and not in Jesus. This was a let- down for me. It really messed my spiritual walk up. My wife and I left the church and started to look for other churches. This church was the only one I knew. It was the only type of service I knew anything about. I didn't know what to do, so I started to pray and seek God for His wisdom.

It turned out that my neighbor was a pastor of the local church near my house. He was an awesome person and read the Bible to me often and taught me scripture in his living room. I would go over to see him many days after work. It was great to have someone teach and disciple me. He never pushed me to come to his church. He did the thing that all Christians need to learn how to do: He loved me right where I was at. His church was a charismatic church and I had never been to a church like that before. I need to admit that the first time I was there and heard people speaking in tongues, I was very freaked out. I did however watch my neighbor, who I trusted, speak in tongues and pray for people. I had never seen an altar opened before at the end of the service for people to go get prayer. It was awesome to see an Acts 2 Church in the present day.

> **Acts 2:1-4** (NKJV)
> 2 When the Day of Pentecost had fully come, they were all with one accord[a] in one place. ² And suddenly there came a sound from heaven, as of a rushing mighty wind, and it filled the whole house where they were sitting. ³ Then there appeared to them divided tongues, as of fire, and *one* sat upon each of them. ⁴ And they were all filled with the Holy Spirit and began to speak with other tongues, as the Spirit gave them utterance.

The gifts flowed and the Holy Spirit poured out, and I was getting touched. My mind and heart had been so closed off to this type of church and now that I opened my heart up to the Lord, He was touching it in ways I did not know existed. At this time my wife was still hurt from our previous experience and was not ready to come regularly with me to church. All this happened so quickly and I was about to find out about another thing that I had no understanding of. I was about to be introduced to the spiritual gift of prophecy. I didn't know much about prophecy or anything to do with it, but I knew I had read about it in scripture.

> **1 Corinthians 14:1** (NLT) speaks about prophecy. It says, "Let love be your highest goal! But you should also desire the special abilities the Spirit gives—especially the ability to prophesy."

The Calling

We had an Evangelist come in for four nights of revival. I had never been to a revival service before, so I took my wife on Sunday morning with me to the church. We ended up in a three hour service. This was awkward for both of us, but I did not want to walk out on him while he was preaching. We had the youth service Sunday night, but I understood that he preached another three hour service! I was really freaked out at this point just hearing about it. I decided to give it another try and go on Tuesday night. I was very nervous to be there and did not know what to expect. The service got started and the worship was awesome. I had never praised and worshipped the Lord like that before in my life. The service was about half way through and the evangelist made his way toward me. He intimidated the living daylights out of me and when he started to walk toward me and I was freaked out. He looked at me and said the following, "I don't know who you are and I have never met you before but God has now spoken to me two times and told me to stop the service and come deliver a word to you. He wants to know why you're not serving him in ministry." I answered with, "I'm scared!" He said, "The Lord wants you to know he is going to send people to help you. He wants you to do what he asked, and we are going to pray for you tonight to follow the call that has been placed on you by God."

The Calling

WOW!!!!! I was now thrust into the fire of ministry and was completely wrecked and could not even cry because I was so mesmerized at what had happened. His team prayed for me and I felt something shift. I am so thankful to him for his obedience to the Lord to deliver the word to me. At the end of the service they had the altar open to worship and get prayer, and of course I went to the altar. As I was on my knees the Lord spoke to me audibly for only me to hear. Here is what He said,

> "Son I have brought you out of a life of sin and have started to transform you in my image. Do not be afraid of what I told you tonight. I will send the people to help you and I will give you the words to speak out of your mouth."

Immediately after that one of the altar workers came up to me and said, "God told me to tell you to read **Jeremiah 1:4-10** (NKJV)," which says,

> 4 Then the word of the Lord came to me, saying: 5 "Before I formed you in the womb I knew you; Before you were born I sanctified you; I ordained you a prophet to the nations." 6 Then said I:"Ah, Lord God! Behold, I cannot speak, for I am a youth." 7 But the Lord said to me: "Do not say, 'I am a youth, 'For you shall go to all to whom I send you, And whatever I command you, you shall speak. 8 Do not be afraid of their faces, For I am with you to deliver you,"

says the Lord. 9 Then the Lord put forth His hand and touched my mouth, and the Lord said to me: "Behold, I have put My words in your mouth. 10 See, I have this day set you over the nations and over the kingdoms, To root out and to pull down, To destroy and to throw down, To build and to plant."

So this was my calling into ministry. I started serving in youth ministry on Sunday nights at our church to get some experience. The pastor was an awesome man of God and did everything he could do to raise me up to answer the call on my life. Until this point I was not on fire for the Lord, but something shifted on Sunday nights. We had three hour services every Sunday night, and I watched teenagers teach me how to worship and hunger for God. I had never seen anything like this before. I watched the youth so hungry for God that I was embarrassed by my lack luster worship and prayer. Sunday nights helped transform me into the man I am today. I stayed almost one year with this group. It was awesome to see what God did to me. I came to serve the youth pastor and just watched this group walk as Jesus did. They showed me how to hunger for the Lord and to seek His presence.

In October of 2008, my wife and I went on a cruise together which was really hard for me now that I knew the Lord. I used to go on cruises to get drunk, smoke cigars, gamble, and go to the adult shows on board the ship. Now I was bored to tears because I was not doing this. Early on in the cruise my wife and I went to a show that had nudity. I have to tell you that I felt dirty watching this show. Thankfully the cruise ship had morning prayer everyday on the boat at 7:30 a.m. I went to the prayer meeting. My wife thought I was nuts again and told me to enjoy my vacation. But I needed to be around some men of God. So I went to the prayer meeting and on a ship of 3500 people, there were only 3 of us that showed up.

> **Matthew 18:20** (NKJV) 20 For where two or three are gathered together in My name, I am there in the midst of them."

The three of us prayed together for about an hour. We really enjoyed the time.

I started to talk to one guy who was really hungry for the Lord as I was. I learned that he lived in Nicaragua and ran a business there and a church as well. He was filled with the word of God. I shared my testimony with him and he shared his with me. It was so cool to meet someone on the ship who was a believer. I asked him what his greatest need was in Nicaragua and he told me that they are always in need of Spanish Bibles. I told him that was great, and that hopefully God would send him some. Little did I know God started planting seeds in my heart.

We got back home and I started to make plans to obey what God had called me to do. I started to work on the plan to open HSGEM which

The Calling

stands for Hawaiian Shirt Guy Evangelism Ministries. I got the name Hawaiian Shirt Guy in the first church I was in because somebody did not know my name and called me the Hawaiian Shirt Guy. Now God was using this to name the ministry He had given me. As more information was downloaded to me by the Lord, I knew He was calling me to Evangelism. This still scared me but I sought the call and did not back down.

In January 2009 I opened the doors of HSGEM Ministries. I did not know what we were going to do with it, but I knew God had called me to preach. I started to study and read the word with more fervency than I ever had. I started to spend time in the presence of the Lord. I just knew he had done something to me and I did not know what happened, but I was not the same guy I used to be.

On January 13th, 2009, on my 35th birthday, I was introduced to the Baptism of the Holy Spirit. I was in Jacksonville on business and I wanted to experience revival again, so I Googled "Revival Jacksonville, FL January 13th." Sure enough a revival service popped up at a local church. I went down there to experience the power of revival. In the past, my birthdays had always been times when I threw keg parties, or we had all night drunken binges in strip clubs, and here I was on my 35th birthday going to experience revival.

When I got there I grabbed a seat. The people were much older than me but I felt comfortable for the moment. The service was moving very quickly and shortly after the evangelist started to preach, the power of God fell on the place and everything shifted. I was on my knees weeping and speaking in tongues for the first time in my life. I was out cold on the floor for about 30 minutes and when I came back to the flesh, there was a man shouting out in tongues and having a conversation with the Lord. There was another man interpreting the tongues.

1 Corinthians 14:5 (NKJV) 5 I wish you all spoke with tongues, but even more that you prophesied; for he who prophesies is greater than he who speaks with tongues, unless indeed he interprets, that the church may receive edification.

I was absolutely in awe of what the Holy Spirit had done that night. I drove back to my hotel and probably got the best night of sleep of my life. I lay in the arms of my heavenly father that night and was completely blessed. After this night my life would never be the same.

My wife, however, did not have an understanding of anything concerning speaking in tongues. In fact she had been taught that it was not of God to speak in tongues, so this really bothered her. Later you will find out that she received the Baptism of the Holy Spirit, and all of her thoughts changed. She used to tell me to turn my music up when I prayed in tongues so she did not have to hear it.

The Calling

By this point I was a full blown Jesus Freak! (Just like the song says). I was enjoying my walk and God was healing me in ways I never knew he could. This was good because I needed a lot of healing after some of the events that had taken place in my life. My wife and I decided to switch churches and start attending a mega church so we could get more training. We had only been at the small charismatic church for a short period of time and my wife needed something different. We went and spoke with a pastor at the mega church. He told us that worship was not supposed to be a spectator sport. This idea was new for Alice. She wanted to know why people raised their hands when they worshipped and why they got excited as she had not experienced this. The pastor spoke some great words of wisdom to us. They were, "Just come with a heart to honor and praise the Lord and let the Holy Spirit do the rest." These words helped lead my wife down a great path of seeking the Lord and allowed her to grow more intimate with God.

We were enjoying being ministered to at this church. Soon we would learn what it was like to serve there. My heart was hungering to serve in this church as I knew how much I enjoyed serving the Lord.

> **1 Corinthians 9:19** (NLT) says, "Even though I am a free man with no master, I have become a slave to all people to bring many to Christ."

The Calling

This verse became a staple of our ministry as I walked down the path on which God had called me. The highpoint of the year happened in March of 2009 when I preached my first sermon at the youth ministry I was serving in on Sunday nights. It was an awesome service. I think I preached myself happy after one hour and 30 minutes of preaching! Earlier in the day, I had been rear ended and the car that hit me took off. When I got out of my car, there was not a scratch on my car. How did this happen? JESUS!

It is so exciting to look back and see what the Lord did in me and for me! Well I have news for you... it's just the start. In the next chapter you will hear what the Lord did with my heart in regards to Spanish Bibles. I promise that you do not want to stop reading.

6 - Bibles, Bibles, & More Bibles

Remember how I told you earlier that I did not have a heart for Spanish Bibles or any Bibles? All of that was about to change as I was thrust into the fire again.

God was giving me a heart for Spanish Bibles. Now something I did not share with you earlier was my experience with the Bible prior to getting saved. It was my second bachelor party before I was getting married. I had been drinking heavily that night and consumed a bottle of crown royal. I was there with two of my friends and they were watching me get crazy in the hotel room before we went out to the strip club. All of a sudden I decided to mock some preachers I had seen on TV. I was carrying on in a drunken tirade, and I grabbed a Bible and held a stick lighter beneath it. I tried to touch the Bible to the lighter so I could burn the Bible. God was not going to have any of this. No matter how hard I tried I was not able to touch the two together. It was very frustrating for me as I really wanted to burn the Bible. You see God loved me enough to prevent

Bibles, Bibles, & More Bibles

me from doing something destructive, even though I did not love him.

1 Timothy 1:13 (NLT) says, "Even though I used to blaspheme the name of Christ. In my insolence, I persecuted his people. But God had mercy on me because I did it in ignorance and unbelief."

I woke up one morning and felt the need to go research what it would cost to purchase some Spanish Bibles. The first Bibles I found were $10.00 apiece and in NKJV translation. Those were full edition and leather bound. I knew the direction we needed to go was paperback as they would be easier to transport. I talked with the guy I had met on the cruise via email and he informed me the best translation was NVI which is Spanish for NIV. He told me this translated the best. I told him I was working on getting some Spanish Bibles to him in Nicaragua to bless him. He was so excited that we were doing this. I got on the phone with some of our ministry supporters and asked them to help us send these Bibles to Central America. In the meantime, I found a full Bible that was paperback and that could be purchased for $3.50 per Bible. We went ahead and raised enough money to send 144 Bibles to Central America in 2009.

Getting the Bibles to Central America is always challenging. Most airlines allow people to take a suitcase that can't weigh more than 50 pounds. Each of these Bibles weighed about five pounds. I had a missionary friend who was going to be moving to Costa Rica with his family. He agreed to take as many as he could. I remember in the days before he left that he needed a suitcase. So we found a suitcase and loaded it up with Bibles for him. Right before he was going to leave the Lord provided the funds to pay for the extra suitcase. These Bibles hit the field instantly and touched many lives. We started to hear reports within the first month about what these Bibles were doing. It was explained to me that in Central America a Bible is very hard to come by. Sometimes they can be as expensive as $150.00 US dollars. Each one of these Bibles would end up ministering to ten or more people. Many families would gather around and read the word of God to each other. This was so touching to know that the 144 Bibles we sent touched 1,440 lives or more. The scriptures tell us to go into the world and make disciples. This is exactly what we were doing by sending these Spanish Bibles.

Matthew 28:19 (NKJV) 19 Go therefore and make disciples of all the nations, baptizing them in the name of the Father and of the Son and of the Holy Spirit.

Of the first amount we were able to send, some of these made their way through Costa Rica and then on to Nicaragua. There was a missionary traveling through Costa Rica and he met one of

Bibles, Bibles, & More Bibles

my friends. He spent some time with him before heading on to Nicaragua and when he was leaving for Nicaragua, he was given a case of Bibles to take. A few weeks later, I received word from that the Bibles had been received. Now some of you are asking why we don't just ship the Bibles to Central America. The main reason is the cost to ship things down there, but another reason is because the government will sometime confiscate them and sell them on the black market. So our model for sending these Spanish Bibles is to find a missionary group going down to Central America and having each person take ten Bibles in the group. This way a group of 20 can take 200 Bibles with them. The new Spanish Bibles we found were $1.00 per piece. They were also lighter and weighed about half a pound each. So a person taking ten would only increase the weight of their bag by five pounds. Most people could find a way to get an additional five pounds in their suitcases. At this point we were about to do some great things with these Bibles because of the things we had learned.

In 2010 we were able to send 106 Spanish Bibles to Central America. Giving was down that year, and I really wanted to send more, but we know that the 106 Spanish Bibles would touch many more lives, so we were obedient and sent them. As we neared the end of 2010 I prayed about how many Bibles we could send in 2011. I thought in the flesh that if we sent 500 we would double the total of 250 we had sent in two years prior. We had an event in January of 2011 that we called "Night of Freedom" to help raise money to send more Spanish Bibles. What happened was miraculous. Many people were healed that night, marriages were saved, and we raised enough money to send 500 Bibles.

> **Luke 16:10-11 (NKJV)** 10 He who *is* faithful in *what is* least is faithful also in much; and he who is unjust in *what is* least is unjust also in much. 11 Therefore if you have not been faithful in the unrighteous mammon, who will commit to your trust the true *riches?*

In 2009 and 2010 we sent 250 Bibles combined. Now in one night in early 2011, we raised enough money to send 500 Bibles. So all of a sudden I needed people to take these Bibles to the mission field for us. I started calling everyone I knew who could take the Bibles for us. However, none of them were heading down there. Out of the clear blue, God spoke audibly to me, and told me to relax and He would send people. The next thing I knew people were calling me about supplying them with Spanish Bibles.

One of the people we were able to work with was a pastor from Jackson, MS. He was taking a team to Costa Rica to meet with some people who I had met a few months earlier. The pastor ended up taking 200 Bibles for us in 2011 to Costa Rica. Later in the year, he took even more Bibles to Mexico for us to the border town of Reynosa.

I wish I could share all of the testimonies with you that I have heard in the short time we have been sending these Bibles. I am going to pick a select few to share with you.

The first is from Costa Rica. A friend of mine and his team ministered to a tribe of Christians called the Waime. They were deep in the jungle in South Costa Rica down near Panama. To get to the tribe they had to make sure they went at the proper time so not to get washed out by the tide. They also had to do this trip with horses to carry the things they needed to bring to the tribe. It was a six to eight hour hike to get up to the tribe. One day they brought some Bibles to them. The chief of the tribe spoke these words, "Pan De Dios." The English translation for this phrase is "Bread from God." When I hear stories like this, it amazes me how something as small as sending Bibles can touch the hearts of so many.

I got to hear from the pastor from Jackson about some Bibles they took to Mexico. They go down to the border town of Reynosa and help build houses for people in Mexico for about one week every year. While the team was down there, they were able to help a deaf school out and bring Bibles to them. It's exciting to hear about the way God uses people to get these Bibles in the proper hands. I was so worried about how we were going to distribute them and God took care of it.

The final story of the testimonies I will share is the story of a friend we will call "David." David partnered with other missionaries to take Bibles in the early days but had returned to the USA to work back here. David decided to go on a mission trip to Costa Rica and Nicaragua. He called me and indicated the need for some Bibles. I got him Bibles and a suitcase and some cash to cover the airline fee for the bag. David took some of these Bibles to Costa Rica and then proceeded to head to Nicaragua. David shared this story with me as he got back. When he left Costa Rica they had to leave the vehicle they were using in Costa Rica. They took the bus into Nicaragua and got off to find their way to find my friend. They started to walk down the road in the hot sun and headed toward their destination. All of a sudden a car came by and offered them a ride. They rode for a while and were dropped off where they could take a bus to the town they were trying to reach. They were able to get to the town and headed to see my friend. When they got there, my friend was down at the beach with his family. David shared with me that they walked down to the beach and told him that they had brought Bibles for him. He was amazed at the hoops they jumped through to get down to Nicaragua. My friend welcomed them and they stayed for a couple days. They had church on Sunday morning and when David and his friend

Bibles, Bibles, & More Bibles

got to the church, they saw some of the Bibles we sent originally two years earlier on the chairs of the church. He said it brought tears to his eyes to see how God had used so many people to get Spanish Bibles in the right place where they were needed.

So we had now raised enough money for 500 Bibles in one night. I thought our work for the year was done, but God would have other ideas about this. About a month after this event in January 2011, God spoke to me and told me we were going to send 1000 more Bibles in 2011 for a total of 1,500. I was blown away but told the Lord to bring it on. It was awesome what the Lord did. We had different people going to many different countries taking Bibles down for us. We ended up sending Bibles to every country in Central America: Belize, Costa Rica, El Salvador, Guatemala, Honduras, Nicaragua, Panama, and Mexico. In addition to this we sent Bibles to Columbia, and Venezuela. We were connected with many people here in the USA because of the work we were doing. I know going forward we will be connected with many more people here that can help us send more and more Bibles each year.

I think my favorite part of the story about the Spanish Bibles is how God took me, a sinner and a man who attempted to burn Bibles, and turned me into a man who has sent them all over the world.

Galatians 2:20 (NKJV) 20 I have been crucified with Christ; it is no longer I who live, but Christ lives in me; and the *life* which I now live in the flesh I live by faith in the Son of God, who loved me and gave Himself for me.

I think we so often put limits on God. I know I have put limits on Him in the past with Spanish Bibles. Finally, I have taken the limits off. My heart is to one day send 150,000 Bibles per year. That is 100 times the amount we sent in 2011.

So often in today's society we forget the value of a dollar. How many things can you purchase for a dollar that can make the impact a Spanish Bible can in a foreign country in Central America? I think it's fitting today that many so called "dollar stores" do not sell many items for one dollar anymore. But for one dollar you can help send the Word of God, Pan De Dios, manna from Heaven to a family that is hungry for the Word of God. "Oh no!" you're saying, "He is going to ask us for money." I am going to ask you to prayerfully consider partnering with us to send these Spanish Bibles. I am asking you to consider how simple it is to change the lives of people in need. I am going to ask you to pray about sowing seed in fertile ground in the Kingdom of God.

If you are interested in helping us, simply go to www.hsgem.org and click on one of the "donate" buttons on any of the pages. They will direct you to a secure site to sow a seed. If you want to let me know you sent a seed for Spanish

Bibles, you can email me at hsgemb@gmail.com and let us know that you're standing with us.

Matthew 9:37 (NKJV) 37 Then He said to His disciples, "The harvest truly is plentiful, but the laborers *are* few.

I hope you have enjoyed reading this chapter, and that you are starting to see the miracles, signs, and wonders the Lord is performing in my life. I want you to start thinking about the miracles, signs, and wonders God has performed in your life as you continue to walk with me on this journey.

7 - The Airport Anointing

The airport is a place I spend a lot of my time. I travel for work and ministry trips and prefer to fly. Shortly after I started traveling again by plane I realized that the airport was a great place to share the Gospel of Jesus Christ. One morning I walked into the airport and felt like I was home. I have a calling to the airport and I am amazed what God does every time I step foot into an airport and on a plane. I realized that each time when I enter the airport I step up onto my pulpit. What you are about to hear in this chapter are stories from my pulpit and the things that have happened in the last three years in the airports I traveled in and on the planes I flew in.

It was September 2009 and I was going to a trade show for work in Nashville, TN. I had a non-stop flight from Orlando to Nashville. This would be a day I will never forget. I was in a really bad mood when I got to the airport and very apprehensive about this trip. I had been with the company I was working for only four months at this time and it had been a very rocky four months. I was going to a major trade show that we had in

The Airport Anointing

Nashville. All of my bosses would be there and co-workers who were just starting to get to know me.

I arrived at the airport very early and had plenty of time to kill. I was sitting in the gate area waiting for the call to board the flight. When I lined up there was a rather friendly guy near me in line. He seemed like he was nice and he said the key word while we were waiting to board the plane. He said, "Blessed." At that point I made a reference to Jesus and the conversation was started. We talked about surface level stuff such as travel and my complaints with airlines. As we were boarding, he asked me if I would like to sit in a row with him and we agreed to sit near each other. I found out soon that his name was Don and he was going to a men's retreat in Nashville later that week. I asked him what church he went to and he told me he went to an Episcopal church in our city. I spoke to the Lord and sarcastically thanked him for putting a boring Episcopal near me on the plane. What came out of his mouth next would make my jaw hit the floor. He told me he had been to the Lakeland Outpouring and spoke in tongues. I had to ask him to repeat himself because I was so shocked at what I just heard. He asked me which part the Episcopal part or the Lakeland outpouring and speaking in tongues. I was absolutely astonished! I had only met one other Spirit filled Episcopalian before.

We had an awesome conversation on our plane ride to Nashville. When the plane landed he did not have any business cards on him so I gave him mine. He told me he would get a hold of me when he got back to Orlando. I was really looking forward to spending more time with Don and getting to know him. There was something I liked about him and I could not figure out what it was. I finally realized that he walked around with the love of Jesus all over him. His heart was to love those who had nobody to love them.

1 Corinthians 13:1-7 (NKJV) 13 Though I speak with the tongues of men and of angels, but have not love, I have become sounding brass or a clanging cymbal. 2 And though I have the gift of prophecy, and understand all mysteries and all knowledge, and though I have all faith, so that I could remove mountains, but have not love, I am nothing. 3 And though I bestow all my goods to feed the poor, and though I give my body to be burned, but have not love, it profits me nothing. 4 Love suffers long *and* is kind; love does not envy; love does not parade itself, is not puffed up; 5 does not behave rudely, does not seek its own, is not provoked, thinks no evil; 6 does not rejoice in iniquity, but rejoices in the truth; 7 bears all things, believes all things, hopes all things, endures all things.

Don and I would go on to be best friends. He would be responsible for many divine appointments later in my walk which you will hear about shortly. I thank God every day for this divine appointment. I would end up having a great trade show and Don would have a great men's retreat. I

The Airport Anointing

believe both of these things took place because of our conversation on the plane and our honoring of Jesus!

In October of 2009 on a plane to Atlanta I would meet Earl. Now this was a very different situation then my meeting with Don. Earl and I would not know that we were going to be best friends until weeks after this flight. Earl was on his way to the Midwest to see one of his sons. He had to change planes in Atlanta. I was on my way to Atlanta for business. It was an early morning flight and I was my usual grumpy self because I do not like getting up at 5 a.m. for anything, let alone to catch a flight. We boarded the plane and found out that our flight was delayed once we were on the plane. This is normal for anything going into Atlanta in the morning due to the low ceiling of visibility there. Earl was sitting in the window seat and I was in the aisle. There was a nice lady in the middle seat between Earl and I. Earl talked with her and I talked with her but we did not talk to each other. The only thing we knew about the other is that we lived ten minutes from each other. All three of us lived in the same part of town. As soon as we hit Atlanta I got off the plane. I don't even remember getting Earl's name when we were on this plane. About three weeks later it was daylight savings time. My wife and I normally went to the 1pm service at our church, but decided to go to the 9 a.m. service at church because we were up early due to the time change. Alice and I

The Airport Anointing

went walking into church and this guy in a suit came up to me and said, "Weren't you on the plane with me to Atlanta a couple weeks ago?" I said, "Yes, I sure was!" He introduced himself as Earl. He was an usher at our church. I asked him how long he had been at that church and he told me 11 years. I had been going there for about a year at the time but had never met him. It was a big church and there were three services so there was a good chance of us not meeting each other.

Once again I had no idea I was to gain another best friend. Earl and I started to hang out and found out that we both had a heart for revival. We both were hungry for the Lord and would follow the Lord wherever he called us to experience revival. We started to travel together and hang out and chase the Holy Ghost together. Earl and I are very opposite people, but we get along so well with each other. It was such an awesome thing that the Lord brought us together.

Good fruit continues to produce good fruit. I had been asking God to give me a spiritual father for most of my walk. I kept thinking I knew who my spiritual father was going to be. I had five men picked out who I wanted to be spiritual fathers to me. Well God had some other plans in that department. All five of the men I picked have left the Lord or fallen in some form of a scandal. Little did I know that Don, the Spirit Filled Episcopalian, would introduce me to my first spiritual father, Charlie. As the friendship continued to build with

The Airport Anointing

Don, he told me that he wanted to introduce me to his friend, Charlie. I met Charlie for the first time in March of 2010. Later on I will talk about Charlie and share the story about the first time I met him.

Back to the airport. I was flying one Sunday to go up to my office for a meeting that I needed to be at Monday morning. When I got to the airport Sunday night the lines were very long to check luggage and check-in for the flight. Because I am a frequent flyer, I went right to the front of the line. A man in the other line was very angry with me and started yelling profanity at me. He then came toward me and approached me. While in the past I would have just decked him, I knew I needed to be a witness to him by my actions and lack of words. I was practicing what Don had showed me which was the love of Jesus. He proceeded to carry on until the airlines employee told him that she would call the police if he did not settle down. I felt bad for him. My heart burdened for him. He was so angry and frustrated that he had to take it out on an innocent traveler. Isn't it interesting how God can grow us in the midst of trying situations?

Another experience I had happened one week when I was flying home from Jackson, MS. after being there to work and to preach. I was exhausted and had a rough week. I was so drained when I got on the plane. My eyes burned from the redness of not sleeping well and I just wanted to be home. A lady came and sat down next to me on the flight. She was very talkative

The Airport Anointing

and I was not happy about this that day. Normally I love someone to talk with on the airplane, but not today. Anyway I was not going to have a choice about this. She was going to talk with me on this flight. I shared with her that I was tired and run down.

She told me that God had sent her to bring me rivers of living water. I asked her who she was and she said, "A Prophet." Her Apostle was sitting right in front of us with another Pastor as well. We talked for the whole flight and she blessed me by reading scripture to me and sharing the prophesy the Lord had given her for me. She was on the way to the ordination of some friends in Maryland and was having to fly through Orlando to get there. Once again God had shown up and showed off. I was so down and tired and I got off the plane and felt on top of the world. God did this so I would be able to go home to my wife refreshed and revived. What an amazing flight that was.

In September of 2011 I had one of my most interesting two flights back to back that I had ever had. I was flying from Indianapolis back to Orlando and had to change planes in Atlanta. On the first flight from Indy to Atlanta I had the honor of ministering to a campaign manager of a well know politician. We were in business class and before the plane could take off the man was drinking hard liquor. He was about 30 years old and had been in politics for quite a while. His father was the education commissioner of a state as well. This

The Airport Anointing

guy proceeded to get completely drunk as fast as he could. He told me he had been in meetings drinking all afternoon as well. He was on his way to Atlanta for a bachelor party for the weekend. Something came out and he shared with me that he was a Christian. I was listening to him and thought that it was definitely the liquor speaking.

He proceeded to tell me about his Christian values. Now I was exhausted as I had been at a trade show all week. I was also getting very frustrated with this guy and his crazy story. Normally I would have waited until Saturday and taken the non-stop flight home but I was ministering Saturday morning and needed to be home Friday night. I asked the Lord what I should do as this drunk would not stop talking. The Lord instructed me to share my testimony with him.

As I started to share my testimony, he could not take his eyes off me. I shared with him for about an hour and then suddenly something awesome happened. As I was wrapping up my testimony his eyes went from complete blood red to white and he went from drunk to sober right before my eyes. This was one of the coolest signs I have ever seen from the Lord. He told me before we exited the plane that he was going to see a friend of his who was a pastor in Atlanta and skip the bachelor party. I gave him one of my business cards and told him to keep in touch with me. I have not heard from him since, but I know the sign

The Airport Anointing

Jesus showed him that night was enough to shake him and change his heart.

Part two of this trip was from Atlanta to Orlando. Now I was very tired by the time I got to the plane as I had to change terminals in Atlanta. It was now about 10pm on a Friday night, and I was ready to go to sleep. As I boarded the plane I noticed there was somebody sitting next to me in business class. The guy who was sitting next to me had started drinking before the plane ever left the gate. It was late, and the airport was jammed, as always. So we had 30 minutes after we left the gate before the plane would take off. I started to talk to this man and he noticed my cross. He asked if I was a Christian, and I confirmed it for him. He told me he was a Catholic and it was perfectly ok for him to get drunk. He told me he was a deacon in his church. I started to share with him the miracles, signs, and wonders I had seen in my life.

At this point he seemed more interested in drinking then listening to my story. I got very frustrated, and I commanded the Holy Spirit to show up, and he did just that. I started to pray for this man in tongues, and I laid my hand on his arm. Within about 20 seconds he was sober as was with the man on the previous plane. The man was amazed. He told me that he believed miracles, signs, and wonders were for the early church and not for today. I spoke to him with authority and boldness and shared the following scripture with him: **Hebrews 13:8** (NKJV) "Jesus Christ *is* the same yesterday, today and forever."

As we walked off the plane, he told me that he had begged God for a sign that he was real for the past six months. He told me that he finally got that sign on the plane. What an awesome blessing this was.

To end this night I would need a miracle myself. When I got near the baggage claim area, my body gave up and quit. I just stopped walking. There was numbness and pain throughout my whole body. I was so tired and did not have anything left. I looked up and there was a Hyatt hotel in the airport and I thought about getting a room there because I literally could not even make it to baggage claim. I knelt down on my hands and knees and cried out for Jesus in the middle of the airport to heal my body so I could get my luggage and get home. Right as I cried out, I felt the numbness go away. My body felt lighter than it had felt. I stood up and said, "Jesus I receive my healing." I walked to baggage claim and got my bag and headed to the parking garage to get my car. I got in my car and headed toward home. I made it home with no problems, and made it to minister the next morning.

I had just witnessed a night of miracles, signs, and wonders. I was completely edified and pumped up. Right before my head hit the pillow that night the Lord spoke to me and told me that my ministry would be defined by miracles, signs, and wonders.

As you can see I have had some journeys in the airports and traveling. Traveling is never dull. People always love to hear the stories of my trips, so I felt that I should share some of them with you. These are just a few of the stories of the airports. There are so many I may decide just to write a whole book on the airport stories.

More importantly at this point of the book, you can start to see what God is using me to do. You can also see how He is changing my heart. You can see that He has thrust me into His fire. Some of you might be asking, "Why doesn't God do these things for me?" I can't answer that as it will most likely be different for every person. However, what I can tell you is that as I fully turned my life over to the Lord and became obedient to the call on my life, He started to move in ways I could not even imagine. I want to challenge you to check in with the Lord and find out where your obedience is. On a scale of 1-10 where is yours? Think about this and see how you can be more obedient to the Lord.

8 - Chasing The Holy Ghost

Up to this point in my spiritual training, I had mostly learned what I needed to know from reading the Bible, being taught by others, serving, and trained in classes. It was now time to get a different form of training than I was used to. I will call this "The School of the Holy Spirit." This was an education which I desperately needed but had not received yet. It was time for God to rock my world! I would be on a mission to get as much time in the presence of the Holy Ghost as possible. I would travel far just to chase true Holy Ghost Revival. I am going to share this journey with you.

In late 2008 and the first part of 2009, I received a great training in the School of the Holy Spirit serving in youth ministry. I remember one evening I was praying for some of the youth, and one young man I'll call "Michael," came up and asked me to pray for him. Michael was 12 years old at the time and on fire for God. At one point, he asked me a question that completely blew me away. Michael asked me to pray the following, "Brad, pray that God will kill me in the flesh and raise me back up in him." I had to step back for a minute and check with him and make sure he knew what he was asking me to pray.

    Have you ever had a time in your life when you realized a 12 year old was closer to God then you were? It really made me think. Michael was asking God to wreck him. He did not care what this looked like, but he knew that more of God and less of him was what he wanted and he was willing to pay the price for this. This completely wrecked me when I heard him say this. It wrecked me even more when I prayed this over him. I was in tears just thinking about what had happened. After I prayed this for Michael I went to the altar myself and sat there and wept and repented. I confessed to the Lord that I needed my attention focused back on him and not on the world.

    By now my hunger for the Holy Ghost was growing daily. I was eager to experience more. I had been baptized in the Holy Ghost and now I just wanted to see the fruits of the spirit and the gifts of the spirit in full effect. I was driving home one day and a friend called and told me that I needed to talk to a pastor friend of hers. She said he was hosting a youth conference and needed some help from ministry leaders and pastors. I got off the phone with her and the Lord told me to call him immediately. I called him and he answered and said to come by his office in ten minutes. I went by his office to visit with him and talk with him. He gave me the details and welcomed me to come join them. I let him know which sessions I could be at which was Friday and Saturday night. I went Friday night and saw some awesome things take place. I knew that Saturday night things were going to be much more intense. I knew we had unfinished business from Friday night.

When we gathered Saturday night at the leaders meeting before hand, we all knew that something awesome was going to happen. There were about 170 youth there at this conference and the Holy Ghost showed up in a mighty way. As the pastor finished preaching his message, he opened the altar and called all the leaders up to pray for people. We formed two lines and faced each other so we could pray for the youth as they walked through. As the first group came through, people started hitting the ground everywhere. This is what is referred to as being slain in the spirit. The next thing I knew there were people falling all over the place. It was all the leaders could do to stay on their feet. We went from falling all over the place to falling all over each other. It got to a point where the leaders were all over the floor as well. I was absolutely in awe of what God had done. I felt an anointing all over me. So much that I went home and laid hands on my wife and also my dog, Fred. Fred really enjoyed this and stayed in my arms. My dog could definitely tell there was something different about Daddy!

As we were at a new church, we noticed right away that the Holy Ghost was present there. It was at this time that I started to learn about deliverance ministry. I kept asking people to tell me about it, but they would not tell me about it. Probably because they knew when I got delivered I would understand more about deliverance. This was another part of the educational journey I was getting in the school of the Holy Spirit. I went to an event called a *God Encounter*. This event changed my life, my walk, and shifted my ministry in a very different direction.

    I went to the *God Encounter* demanding that God show up and heal me, and He did. I was dealing with many issues at this time but most specifically issues with lust. The *God Encounter* started on a Friday night and ended on a Sunday afternoon. Now remember I told you about Michael who asked me to pray that crazy prayer? Well Friday night I re-dedicated my life to the Lord and as we were in a time of prayer and I was on my face on the floor, I asked the Lord what to pray. This was the first time I had ever asked the Lord what to pray. He responded with telling me to pray what Michael asked me to pray. So I did as I said, "God kill me in my flesh and raise me back up in you." At that point I felt a release like I had never felt before. During the weekend I would experience a time of great healing, deliverance, and time in the presence of the Lord. I would later go on to serve at many *God Encounters*, and I was always touched at each one to see what the Holy Spirit would do when I allowed him and welcomed him into my life. I saw plenty of power and miracles, signs, and wonders take place.

The next part of this training for me was when I started to spend time with Charlie, my first spiritual father. I had wanted a spiritual father for so long and then God tried to give me one, and I just about pushed him away. When I first met Charlie I thought he was an arrogant jerk. The first time I met him he told me a story about how God gave him a Harley and a Rolex. I was thinking to myself, "Who is this wacko?" I called my friend, Don, back and told him that Charlie was nuts and I did not want to spend any time with him. Don made me promise to go see Charlie again. So I did. The next time was very different. I knew Charlie was a prophet, and expected some things to come out when I went to see him. This was part of why I was so scared of him.

Matthew 10:41 (NKJV) 41 He who receives a prophet in the name of a prophet shall receive a prophet's reward. And he who receives a righteous man in the name of a righteous man shall receive a righteous man's reward.

Charlie called some things out that night when we were talking after the Bible study. He asked me what was going on with my dad, and I told him I did not like my dad. He told me the story of himself and his struggles with his dad. He told me that I needed to love my dad as the Bible instructed me to do. He told me that I did not need to agree with the things he was doing, but I must love him. He told me to go practice that. Well I actually listened to him and went to practice loving my father. I knew Charlie had something I wanted but did not know what it was.

I went back to see him two weeks later. He asked me what had been going on with my dad and I told him I loved him, as the Lord told me to.

The day before, the Lord had told me to go see Charlie about being my spiritual father. So during the Bible study he called my name and told me to get up and share my testimony for five to seven minutes. As I was doing this I felt the anointing come on me. I was so thankful to have that opportunity that night. As I sat down Charlie asked what I was doing that Sunday night, and I said I did not have plans. He asked me to come preach at Oxpen Ministries which was a place to get some pulpit time in a safe environment. He told me to prepare a message 15 minutes long and that I would be critiqued.

After Bible study was over Charlie told me the Lord told him to father me. I told him that the Lord had told me to come see him about fathering me as well. I was so happy. Something I had been searching for was finally given to me. Interestingly the Lord gave me Charlie not when I wanted or when I thought I was ready, but when He wanted and He knew I was ready. I know so often we want God to show up and do things but he is really waiting for us to be ready to receive what He is going to do. We must prepare a table before him and be ready to receive him.

Psalm 23:5 (NKJV) 5 You prepare a table before me in the presence of my enemies; You anoint my head with oil; My cup runs over.

I remember the Sunday night when I preached Oxpen. I was so nervous and scared because I did not want to disappoint Charlie. I still lived under the belief that I had to earn God's love, which is completely contrary to what His Word says.
John 3:16 (NKJV) 16 For God so loved the world that He gave His only begotten Son, that whoever believes in Him should not perish but have everlasting life.

The worship leader was leading us into a place of deep worship and praise of the Lord. It was much deeper then I had gone before. I had a few others preaching with me that night who were much more seasoned then I was. I remember preaching a great message that night. God had given me a word and I received some good critiques after the message. Before the critiques though we had a time where we opened the altar because the presence of the Holy Ghost was there in the sanctuary with us.
I remember Charlie sent this guy over for me to pray with. This guy was smelly and sweaty and looked like a bum. I did not know who he was. I started to pray for him and he pulled on my

prophetic gift and asked me to share with him what the Lord was showing me. As I did this, his eyes lit up, because he knew what I was telling him was from God. This was really cool. He hugged me and went back to his seat. I thought for sure that Charlie had set me up to see where my heart was. I would find out later that the man was an elder in that church, owned a landscaping business and came in late because he was working. I also found out that he was a prophet. I would find out in the coming weeks that he was envious of me and he did not like the fact that I was hanging around Charlie. You must be careful when you start talking bad about men and women who are called to serve God. He stayed angry at me for a few weeks, but finally went to the Lord and repented for his dislike of me. What did God do with this? Well, God gave him a heart for me that he never knew existed. He loved me unconditionally like a brother, and we still to this day enjoy a wonderful friendship. Nothing either of us can say to each other will drive us away from each other. It's a friendship ordained by God himself.

    Charlie spent a lot of time with me. He took me under his wing and set out to teach me everything I would allow him to. He brought me into a new realm of the Holy Ghost that I did not know existed. He taught me about the prophetic, and showed me about the Apostolic and the 5-fold ministry gifts.

Ephesians 4:11-15 (NKJV) 11 And He Himself gave some *to be* apostles, some prophets, some evangelists, and some pastors and teachers, 12 for the equipping of the saints for the work of ministry, for the edifying of the body of Christ,13 till we all come to the unity of the faith and of the knowledge of the Son of God, to a perfect man, to the measure of the stature of the fullness of Christ; 14 that we should no longer be children, tossed to and fro and carried about with every wind of doctrine, by the trickery of men, in the cunning craftiness of deceitful plotting, 15 but, speaking the truth in love, may grow up in all things into Him who is the head—Christ.

Most importantly, Charlie taught me about Fathers and Sons. The reason he told me to love my father was so that I could learn how to be a son. I could not receive the love of the Father until I knew how to be a son. Learning how to be a son was one of the hardest but most rewarding things that I have ever gone through in my life. The other main thing I needed to learn about fathers and sons, was inheritance. I had no clue about this as my earthly father had never talked to me about this. I went to the Bible to see what my Heavenly Father said about this.

Luke 15:11-32 (NKJV) 11 Then He said: "A certain man had two sons. 12 And the younger of them said to his father, 'Father, give me the portion of goods that falls to me.' So he divided to them his livelihood. 13 And not many days after, the younger son gathered all together, journeyed to a far country, and there wasted his possessions with prodigal living. 14 But when he had spent all, there arose a severe famine in that land, and he began to be in want. 15 Then he went and joined himself to a citizen of that country, and he sent him into his fields to feed swine. 16 And he would gladly have filled his stomach with the pods that the swine ate, and no one gave him anything. 17 "But when he came to himself, he said, 'How many of my father's hired servants have bread enough and to spare, and I perish with hunger! 18 I will arise and go to my father, and will say to him, "Father, I have sinned against heaven and before you, 19 and I am no longer worthy to be called your son. Make me like one of your hired servants."' 20 "And he arose and came to his father. But when he was still a great way off, his father saw him and had compassion, and ran and fell on his neck and kissed him. 21 And the son said to him, 'Father, I have sinned against heaven and in your sight, and am no longer worthy to be called your son.' 22 "But the father said to his servants, 'Bring out the best robe and put it on him, and put a ring on his hand and sandals on his feet. 23 And bring the fatted calf here and kill it, and let us eat and be merry; 24 for this my son was dead and is alive again; he was lost and is found.' And they began to be merry. 25 "Now his older son was in the field. And as he came and drew near to the house, he heard music and dancing. 26 So he called one of the servants and asked what these things meant. 27 And he said to him, 'Your brother has come, and because he has received him safe and sound, your father has killed the fatted calf.' 28 "But he was angry and would not go in. Therefore his father came out and pleaded with him. 29 So he answered and said to his father, 'Lo, these many years I have been serving you; I never transgressed your commandment at any time; and yet you never gave me a young goat, that I might make merry with my friends. 30 But as soon as this son of yours came, who has devoured your livelihood with harlots, you killed the fatted calf for him.'31 "And he said to him, 'Son, you are always with me, and all that I have is yours. 32 It was right that we should make merry and be glad, for your brother was dead and is alive again, and was lost and is found.'"

This story explains it all to us. This is what Charlie was trying to teach me the whole time I was with him. It would take a lot of pounding it into my head to get me to understand this. I finally learned the difference between a father-son relationship and a mentor-mentee relationship. The father gives his son his inheritance.

I finally realized that our Heavenly Father loves us so much that he pours it all out on us. He gives us everything. This is one of the reasons He sends the Holy Spirit to us. The Lord wants us to spend time in his presence. He wants us to feel His tangible presence in our daily walk with Him. I am so blessed by the Holy Spirit and have one major desire which is to experience more of the Holy Ghost. Where are you at with the Holy Ghost? Is He random to you or do you wake up with Him every day?

9 - California Dreaming

I spent a lot of vacations in Southern California when I was growing up. My dad lived in the Los Angeles area, and I would fly out there from Orlando to visit him. The times I would spend out there would be great times. I loved the climate and the weather. I also enjoyed that you could be at the beach swimming and two hours later could be in the mountains skiing.

I would travel out to Los Angeles on and off before I was saved. My dad was still living there at the time. I took a trip there in September of 2001. I was still married to my first wife at the time, and I took a trip to show her Los Angeles and Orange County. We had a good time driving around Southern California on that trip. I was not saved yet and the trip was my last one to California before I got saved. At the end of that trip is when I lost my Nana Sadie. I was on the way to the airport early in the morning on Labor Day to fly home when I got the phone call that she had passed during the night. It was a day I will never forget. It was a long trip home and the five and a half hour flight seemed to take all day. I was relieved to finally get off the airplane and go see my mom.

The next trip I took to California was in March of 2009. I had been saved at this point and baptized in the Holy Ghost. I went to California to spend a weekend with my cousin, Cheryl. Little did I know what God had in store for this weekend in Los Angeles.

I arrived on a Thursday night. The weekend was filled with some amazing things. I decided that I needed to make a trip to Azusa Street in Los Angeles where the 1906 Revival took place that was a catalyst for the spread of Pentecostalism in the USA. When I got there I had a hard time locating where anything had taken place. Today the only physical remain of this revival is a small blue street sign that identifies that portion of Azusa Street as a place where the 1906 revival took place. However, as I got out of my car I felt something else happening. I knew that this was holy ground I stood on. I could feel the presence of the Holy Spirit there and knew that even 103 years later and many buildings being built, that the grounds were still hallowed. I walked around for a little while before I departed. It was a real treasure to spend some time there, and I am so glad I was finally able to go to this site.

On this trip, I wanted to experience revival as much as I could. I had prayed about where we should go and sought the Lord's guidance on where to stop and where to worship. On a

California Dreaming

Saturday night, I felt the Lord leading my cousin and me to attend a Saturday night service at Faith Community Church in West Covina, Ca. As we got there I knew something special was going to happen that night. My cousin and I took a seat near the front of the sanctuary.

As the service started I noticed some staff from TBN were sitting in the front row of the sanctuary. I could anticipate at this point that we were not going to have a regular church service that night. The worship was amazing and we could feel the presence of the Lord in the building. At that point, Arthur Blessit was announced and came out with his big Cross that he had carried all over the world. Arthur was in Southern California as they were about to release his new movie called *The Cross* at Grauman's Chinese Theater in Hollywood, CA. During this service I felt the Lord's hand on my shoulder throughout the service. I kept looking around to see who had put their hand on my shoulder, and nobody physically had put their hand on my shoulder. It was an amazing thing that was taking place. In addition I could see my cousin was really getting touched as Arthur shared his stories of taking the cross all over the world with us. It was absolutely incredible to hear. I made sure the next week when the movie was released that I went out to see it. My cousin and I were both touched that evening in so many different ways. I never knew until after the service why God had sent me there. Just before we left, I was waiting for my cousin and I was able to talk with Arthur Blessit for a moment. He prayed a blessing over me before he walked away. It was a night I will never forget.

On this trip we also made a special stop at the Crystal Cathedral and walked around the grounds. The grounds were absolutely amazing. They had a large bell tower in which we went to pray. Around the grounds there were scriptures imbedded on stones, and they were all over the place. It was nice to walk the grounds and read scriptures. There were statues of different scenes from the Bible and also of different people from the Bible. The statue that stuck out to me the most was that of Jesus walking on the water. It had a statue of Jesus in the middle of a pond walking on the water as it is talked about in the book of Matthew.

> **Matthew 14:22-33** (NKJV) 22 Immediately Jesus made His disciples get into the boat and go before Him to the other side, while He sent the multitudes away. 23 And when He had sent the multitudes away, He went up on the mountain by Himself to pray. Now when evening came, He was alone there. 24 But the boat was now in the middle of the sea, tossed by the waves, for the wind was contrary. 25 Now in the fourth watch of the night Jesus went to them, walking on the sea. 26 And when the disciples saw Him walking on the sea, they were troubled, saying, "It is a ghost!" And they cried out for

fear. 27 But immediately Jesus spoke to them, saying, "Be of good cheer! It is I; do not be afraid." 28 And Peter answered Him and said, "Lord, if it is You, command me to come to You on the water." 29 So He said, "Come." And when Peter had come down out of the boat, he walked on the water to go to Jesus. 30 But when he saw that the wind *was* boisterous, he was afraid; and beginning to sink he cried out, saying, "Lord, save me!" 31 And immediately Jesus stretched out *His* hand and caught him, and said to him, "O you of little faith, why did you doubt?" 32 And when they got into the boat, the wind ceased. 33 Then those who were in the boat came and worshiped Him, saying, "Truly You are the Son of God."

At this point all I could do is weep. Two and a half years earlier I did not know who Jesus was and now this whole trip was spent experiencing His goodness and being taught in depth about who He was.

There is one last part of this trip that really sticks out at me. On Sunday morning we decided to go worship at the Angeles Temple, which was the Church that was connected to the LA Dream Center. I was in for a huge surprise. I had read about the dream center and their work to get people off of Skid Row and also off of drugs and alcohol. We arrived there about 30 minutes early on a Sunday morning and had a hard time finding a parking spot. I kept seeing more and more busses outside the building. What I found out is that most of the members there were buses in from Skid Row, the Dream Center, and rehab programs throughout downtown LA. The building was large and historic as it was built in 1923. It holds 5,300 people and we found our way to the third floor to find some seats. To this point I had attended mostly white country club churches that were in middle to upper class sections of town. Now I was standing in a multicultural church in downtown LA that had people from every walk of life in attendance that day. A verse of scripture came to me as I was standing there and this would later change my ministry and my life.

Matthew 6:33 (NKJV) 33 But seek first the kingdom of God and His righteousness, and all these things shall be added to you.

What I was witnessing was a true representation of the Kingdom of God. After this trip my wife and I made the decision to join a multicultural church. A church that represented the Kingdom of God where everybody worshiped together and race and skin color had no bearing. We were all one as members of the Kingdom of God. This was a trip I will never forget as there were many highlights. God changed so many things in my life on this trip and it was so impactful.
    I would go back to Los Angeles with my wife, Alice, in September of 2010. This trip was very different than the previous trip. It would be a trip where the Lord would ask me to rest. This is

very hard for me. I am a type A personality and I usually go about 1,000 miles an hour until I hit the wall. My wife and I went to Burbank first and then to Dana Point. The Lord asked me to rest, turn off my email, Facebook, and Twitter for this trip. So I did! What an amazing trip we had. We spent time relaxing and got to rest.

> **Matthew 11:28-30** (NKJV) 28 Come to Me, all *you* who labor and are heavy laden, and I will give you rest. 29 Take My yoke upon you and learn from Me, for I am gentle and lowly in heart, and you will find rest for your souls. 30 For My yoke *is* easy and My burden is light."

We spent time driving along the coast, enjoying good restaurants, swimming in the pool at our hotels, and of course watching sunsets. The coolest part of this trip was the blessings the Lord bestowed upon us. We knew going on this trip that money was tight. I had wanted to bring a minimal amount of spending money on the trip, and the Lord kept telling me to bring a specific amount much greater than I wanted. I finally stopped fighting and brought the amount the Lord told me to. We enjoyed ourselves and spent most of the money we had brought. The day before we were supposed to go home, we checked our bank account. To our amazement the exact amount of money the Lord told me to take on the trip was deposited in our bank account. It was an unexpected bonus from work. Thank You Jesus! Just wait, it gets better.

I had rested as God had requested. I had been obedient and was very relaxed when I came home. I got back to work the next day after getting home, and found out I needed to plan a trip to my corporate office in Wisconsin to meet some of my customers there for a factory tour in late September. I had wanted to go to World Revival Church in Kansas City, MO for over a year and the Lord had never let me go. Remember in the previous chapter I said I was chasing the Holy Ghost? Well as you can see now I was chasing Holy Ghost Revival.

As I planned this trip to Wisconsin, I got the word from the Lord to book my trip to Kansas City to go to World Revival Church for one Friday night on the way back home to Orlando. The Lord told me it was because of my obedience in the rest he requested that he allowed me to go. He also told me I was ready to receive what World Revival Church had for me. I did not know that I had not been ready to receive. I understood this more after I left there.

I went Friday night just expecting God to show up. I had never been in a service like this before. Eight hundred people were raising their hands and worshiping together with a hunger for the Lord. His presence in the place was thick. There would be a young pastor who was slain in the spirit early in the service. Later I would find out that there was a connection. Pastor Steve preached an awesome message about Revival and I knew I was in Revival. I went to the front as soon as he was done to get prayer and ended up on the ground. I kept getting up and others would come pray for me and I continued to receive. Finally after getting off the ground for the third time I went to find the pastor. The Lord told me to take him to dinner and have fellowship with him. As I shared this with him, we were both whisked into a room and fed with an amazing spread of food. We left there and both went back to our respective hotels. I thought I would never see him again.

    The next morning as I walked into the Kansas City airport, the first person I saw was the pastor. We ate breakfast together before we left. We found out we were on the same flight going to Atlanta and changing planes. As we were in the gate area the Lord directed me to bless him. I went to the gate agent and asked if we could both be bumped up to business class. She was happy to do that for us, and we got to sit next to each other on the plane in business class to Atlanta. I will never forget what happened next. The flight attendant came over to us and asked us who we were. She told us that she had heard us talking. The pastor said, "He is an Evangelist, and I am a Pastor, and I believe we are supposed to pray for you." She said she had been in a spirit-filled church for 20 years and was struggling with fear. We prayed for her for about 10 minutes, at one point I turned around and people behind us had their arms stretched out to her as we were praying for her. We got off the plane and he and I went our separate ways. To this day we still keep in touch and talk often and have made plans to get together sometime in 2012 as there is a bond from the revival time we spent together.

My final trip in this chapter to California was in March of 2012. I took my wife once again on this trip, and it was a combination of work and vacation. The first part of the trip we spent in Newport Beach resting on the California Coast. The first day I was there I woke up and the Lord told me he was going to write some new history for me in California. As a young man I enjoyed time on Balboa Island. Early Saturday morning I went to a Barber shop on the island. The Lord kept telling me that there was going to be someone to minister to in the Barber Shop, and when I got there it was just me and the barber. He is an old school barber in his late 60's, and I came to find out that he had a strong relationship with Jesus. I did not pick-up on it when I walked in the door, but he was the one I was there to minister to. I shared my testimony with him as he gave me a hot towel shave. This was such a great time.

The next day my wife and I drove to Las Vegas for our work meeting. I spent four days in Vegas and could not wait to get out of there. We finally left there on Thursday and headed to Santa Monica for four more days of rest. My plan for the trip was to start writing this book. But, once again, God had another plan which was for me to rest and start the book when I got home. So I rested.

I coined a new term out of this trip for "R and R". Rest and Relaxation = Revelation

As I continue to take times of rest, the Lord reveals the things to me that I have been waiting for.

I want you to take a few things away from this chapter. The first is that God can take things and places of the past and make new memories out of them as he did for me with Southern California. The second is obedience to the Lord. As you just read in this chapter, so many times I had the chance to be disobedient, but I was not. Because of my obedience there were many things God was able to do. The final thing I want you to gain is that when the Lord calls you to rest, it's time to rest. Look at the things that happened as I rested on these trips. California is a place that is near and dear to my heart. I am honored and blessed to have been able to share my experiences from California with you.

10 - Speak Lord! Your Servant Is Listening!

In December of 2011, the Lord called me by four names in this order: Jeremiah, Samuel, David, and Benjamin. I shared previously about Jeremiah and how the Lord used the story of Jeremiah to call me to Ministry. In this chapter I am going to share about Samuel and how the Lord has used Samuel to teach me things. I really started exploring this scripture more in September of 2011 when I heard it preached, although I had been having experiences like this my entire walk, when I heard this passage, it was a confirmation to me that it was the Lord I had been hearing.

> **1 Samuel 3:1-20** (NKJV) 3 Now the boy Samuel ministered to the Lord before Eli. And the word of the Lord was rare in those days; there was no widespread revelation. 2 And it came to pass at that time, while Eli was lying down in his place, and when his eyes had begun to grow so dim that he could not see, 3 and before the lamp of

Speak Lord! Your Servant Is Listening!

God went out in the tabernacle of the Lord where the ark of God *was,* and while Samuel was lying down, 4 that the Lord called Samuel. And he answered, "Here I am!" 5 So he ran to Eli and said, "Here I am, for you called me." And he said, "I did not call; lie down again." And he went and lay down. 6 Then the Lord called yet again, "Samuel!" So Samuel arose and went to Eli, and said, "Here I am, for you called me." He answered, "I did not call, my son; lie down again." 7 (Now Samuel did not yet know the Lord, nor was the word of the Lord yet revealed to him.) 8 And the Lord called Samuel again the third time. So he arose and went to Eli, and said, "Here I am, for you did call me." Then Eli perceived that the Lord had called the boy. 9 Therefore Eli said to Samuel, "Go, lie down; and it shall be, if He calls you, that you must say, 'Speak, Lord, for Your servant hears.'" So Samuel went and lay down in his place. 10 Now the Lord came and stood and called as at other times, "Samuel! Samuel!"
And Samuel answered, "Speak, for Your servant hears." 11 Then the Lord said to Samuel: "Behold, I will do something in Israel at which both ears of everyone who hears it will tingle. 12 In that day I will perform against Eli all that I have spoken concerning his house, from beginning to end. 13 For I have told him that I will judge his house forever for the iniquity which he knows, because his sons made themselves vile, and he did not restrain them. 14 And therefore I have sworn to the house of Eli

that the iniquity of Eli's house shall not be atoned for by sacrifice or offering forever."
15 So Samuel lay down until morning, and opened the doors of the house of the Lord. And Samuel was afraid to tell Eli the vision. 16 Then Eli called Samuel and said, "Samuel, my son!" He answered, "Here I am." 17 And he said, "What is the word that the Lord spoke to you? Please do not hide it from me. God do so to you, and more also, if you hide anything from me of all the things that He said to you." 18 Then Samuel told him everything, and hid nothing from him. And he said, "It is the Lord. Let Him do what seems good to Him." 19 So Samuel grew, and the Lord was with him and let none of his words fall to the ground. 20 And all Israel from Dan to Beersheba knew that Samuel had been established as a prophet of the Lord.

Early on in my walk I heard the voice of the Lord audibly. This was taking place even before I was called to ministry. Some people close to me today are still in amazement of how clearly I hear from the Lord. Most of my friends or people I come in contact with think that this gift is a wonderful thing to have. It is! What I want to share with you are the experiences I have had and the things the Lord has spoken to me over the years.

In the first three weeks of my walk I was told by the Lord to leave the business I was a co-owner of. This was my first experience with hearing from the Lord. I called a friend of mine who was a mature Christian and asked him to help me make sure this was the Lord calling me and not the enemy. After prayer and discernment we knew that this was the Lord. So I was obedient and listened and made plans to leave the business. I did not know what I would do for work, I just knew that God would take care of me. Or at least that's all I had to stand on at that point. I remember reading the scripture about Samuel and the Lord speaking to him. The business I was an owner in was having serious financial troubles at the time the Lord told me to step away. We could barely make payroll every couple of weeks. As soon as I announced my decision, a shift took place. I stayed on for three more months until I was able to get another job. During this period, every two weeks we would have enough money to make payroll. So many times the night before we would not have the money and the next day a check would come in and cover the payroll. It was an awesome thing to see what God was doing. It really built my faith. I took a job that I knew nothing about. The company I went to work for offered to train me for five weeks and teach me the business. I did not want to take the job but the Lord told me he would get me through it. It did not take long until the Lord made me an expert in the industry and I knew my products very well and was able to be a real asset to my customers. When the Lord first told me all of this, I was like

Speak Lord! Your Servant Is Listening!

Samuel and did not know it was the Lord speaking to me.

In May of 2010 my wife was in a very bad car accident. She fractured her pelvis in five places and was to be on the couch or bed rest for the next six months. Early in June of 2010 the Lord gave me a word for my wife. The word was that on August 19, 2010, she would not be able to sleep and there would be a shift that would take place and that she would never be the same again, and that she would hunger for the Lord like she had never hungered for the Lord before. A couple of months later I was woken up about 2:45 a.m. and Alice told me she could not sleep. I went to the calendar and it was August 19th. I went to my journal and read the word the Lord had given me. We lay in bed and talked for quite a while. At 7 a.m. when I went to get up the anointing was so strong coming from Alice. The presence of the Lord was so thick in the room that I was unable to move. I just stayed there in the presence of the Lord and watched as my wife was visibly moved by the Lord. After this experience her healing was accelerated and less than a month later she was driving again, something we did not think she would do so soon. You see, when the Lord told me this I did not want to share this with my wife, but I had to be obedient to the Lord and the word He gave me.

At one point, the Lord gave me a word for a friend of mine. The word was that my friend was in rebellion and needed to repent. It was a harsh word to deliver. I did not want to deliver it. I was arguing with the Lord about calling my friend and sharing the word with him. This time there was another step other than just delivering the word. I was supposed to walk with my friend and help him through this time and help him walk out of rebellion and back into the arms of God. God had told me to lead him out of the bondage. I was so scared. I turned to this verse and allowed the Lord to minister to me.

Proverbs 17:11 (NKJV) 11 An evil man seeks only rebellion; Therefore a cruel messenger will be sent against him.

I called my friend on a Saturday morning and left him a message and told him I had a word for him from the Lord. He decided that he needed to wait until Monday to hear the word. I woke up Sunday morning and the Lord told me to call him and deliver the word. I told the Lord he did not want to hear it and the Lord continued to tell me to deliver the word. So I called my friend. I shared with him the word the Lord had given me. I knew he was angry on the other end of the phone. I did exactly what the Lord had told me. I told him to pray about it and seek the Lord and allow Him to minister to him. He called me back on Monday and let me know he had been in rebellion for the last several months. He asked for my help getting out of rebellion. I told him I would walk this out with him. He pulled out of this period of rebellion in the weeks following the word. The thought that hit me was what if I was disobedient and did not follow what the Lord had called me to do? How many people might this have affected?

    I was in Charleston, SC for a short time in November of 2010 to visit some family. I was looking for a place to go worship on a Sunday morning. I kept looking through the internet and phone book for the right place for me to attend. I just did not feel like anything I had come upon was the place I was supposed to be. Finally on Saturday, the Lord woke me up from a nap and told me to go search the internet again and told me what to type in the search bar. I typed what he told me and found what looked like an awesome church right near where we were staying. I read the bio of the Pastor and knew that's where I was supposed to go. I also noticed that a worship leader who I knew was there the week before. So I prepared myself to go on Sunday morning, and as I got ready I had second thoughts. I knew that God had told me to go there and pushed through and went.

    When I got there, I was a little nervous because I did not know anybody. When the worship started I immediately felt the presence of the Holy Spirit in the sanctuary. The next thing I know, the Holy Spirit completely took over. The pastor was drunk in the spirit and could hardly stand. I was weeping and in amazement at what was taking place. Miracles, signs, and wonders took place there that day. Had I not been obedient and listened to the Lord I would never have experienced what I did. In addition to this, the pastor and I connected and are still in each others lives today. It was awesome. God knew exactly what I needed, and I knew that indeed He had spoken to me.

I met a friend of mine for dinner one night and we had a great time together. We had not seen each other in about a year and we enjoyed catching up. He is an awesome man of God and his conversation completely blessed me. I went back to my hotel room and went to bed later that evening. About 4:30am the Lord woke me with a word for my friend. Now understand that when I am asleep I do not want to be woken up by the Lord or anybody else. I finally fell back to sleep and about 5:20 a.m. I heard the Lord again. Finally at 5:30 a.m., I woke up and said, "Speak Lord for your servant is listening." The Lord started to speak and I started to write.

I wrote the word the Lord gave me for him. Once again a word I did not want to share with my friend but a word the Lord called me to share with him. The Lord also told me to walk this word out with him and help him walk it out. I can gladly say today that he and his wife are walking this out and answering the call of God on their lives.

Often the Lord has called me to preach a word of correction to the church. This is always the hard part. As with most people today, we want others to like us. So here is the dilemma: preach of yourself and have people like you, or be obedient to the Lord and preach what he tells you. I made a decision in January 2009 that I would obey the Lord and preach what he asked me. One evening I was called by the Lord to bring a word of forgiveness to a church. This was hard for me to deliver. It was even harder when I walked in and saw in the spirit that there were many people holding un-forgiveness toward each other. As I started to preach, I felt that I was releasing healing over the church body. I preached for about 45 minutes and released what the Lord told me to release. When I was done, nobody stayed around to talk with me. They all left and headed home early. I was on the road and spent the night in my hotel room feeling lonely and wondering if I did the right thing. The next morning the Lord sent an apostle and a prophet to sit next to me on the plane to minister to me on the way home. It was awesome. When I arrived home, I had a voicemail from the pastor telling me that he had people lined up in his office that morning, telling him they needed to forgive their brothers and sisters. WOW! Little did I know how God would use my obedience.

Another instance of God telling me to preach a corrective word was when I was called to preach **Isaiah 58:6-14** in a friend's church. I was to preach both a corrective and an encouraging word.

> **Isaiah 58:6-14 (NLT)** 6 "No, this is the kind of fasting I want: Free those who are wrongly imprisoned; lighten the burden of those who work for you. Let the oppressed go free, and remove the chains that bind people. 7 Share your food with the hungry, and give shelter to the homeless. Give clothes to those who need them, and do not hide from relatives who need your help. 8 "Then your salvation will come like the dawn, and your wounds will quickly heal. Your godliness will lead you forward, and the glory of the Lord will protect you from behind. 9 Then when you call, the Lord will answer. 'Yes, I am here,' he will quickly reply. "Remove the heavy yoke of oppression. Stop pointing your finger and spreading vicious rumors! 10 Feed the hungry, and help those in trouble. Then your light will shine out from the darkness, and the darkness around you will be as bright as noon. 11 The Lord will guide you continually, giving you water when you are dry and restoring your strength. You will be like a well-watered garden, like an ever-flowing spring. 12 Some of you will rebuild the deserted ruins of your cities. Then you will be known as a rebuilder of walls and a restorer of homes. 13 "Keep the Sabbath day holy. Don't pursue your own interests on that day, but enjoy the Sabbath and speak of it with delight as the Lord's holy day. Honor the Sabbath in everything you

do on that day, and don't follow your own desires or talk idly. 14 Then the Lord will be your delight. I will give you great honor and satisfy you with the inheritance I promised to your ancestor Jacob. I, the Lord, have spoken!"

The awesome thing was the grace God gave me to deliver this word. This word had been birthed in me ten months earlier, but the Lord was waiting for the right time to tell me to deliver this word. They received it and used it to go to the next level as God had called them to.

The final story I will share in this chapter goes back to Samuel and Samuel telling the Lord to speak; that his servant was listening. I had heard this message preached on a Sunday evening and it really moved me. It was a strong word for me to hear. It really represented my walk with the Lord. So I went on the road that week and on Wednesday night I was asking the Lord where I was supposed to preach.

So at 5 p.m. he sat me in the car and told me to drive. I drove around for one and a half hours until I finally ended up near a church I knew. I was hungry at this point and there was a convenience store with a restaurant in it, and I stopped there to eat. Down the road from the convenience store was the county jail. As I was eating a young lady came in that had just been released from the jail. The Lord directed me to minister to her. It took about five minutes and she asked me to lead her in a prayer of salvation. I did and she was saved. She walked out of the store with her head held high and a smile on her face. I went over to the church that I knew of nearby. As the service started the pastor asked people to share their testimony, and I shared mine. He asked me to come preach the next time I was in town. I did so, and the Lord called me to preach **1 Samuel 3:1-10** which says,

> "When the Lord calls you, answer his call. The Lord is looking for a church full of Samuels. He is looking for an army of believers that will say, "Speak Lord! Your servant is listening."

11 - Triumphant Faith

In January of 2007, when I was saved, my life was in shambles. Things felt like they could only get worse. The only thing I had to stand on was Jesus. At this time my faith was weak. I did believe in Jesus and the things he had done, but I still wasn't sure that I was ready to trust Him to do the things the Word of God promised. It was at this time that the Lord spoke to me and told me to give him the five things that I believed were impossible to change and repair, and in the next five years he would fix all of them for me. I want you to see that the number five is going to come into play again in these final chapters. In the story of David and Goliath (1 Samuel 17:1-58) David had five stones to kill Goliath, but only used one. More importantly David's victory over Goliath came from triumphant faith.

The first thing I asked the Lord to fix was my marriage. When I came to know the Lord my marriage was on the verge of being over. My wife and I didn't like each other anymore, but we were still in love with each other. I truly did not believe the Lord could heal my marriage. You can ask the Lord to do things all day long, but you must play your part and believe that he can change them. It's not for you and I to wish against these things, or to continue to get in the way of the Lord, it's for us to co-labor with him. **1 Corinthians 3:9** (NKJV) 9 For we are God's fellow workers; you are God's field, you are God's building.

As God started to change my heart for my wife, something shifted in our marriage. I went from being in a place of where I felt that being married to Alice was a burden, to a place where I wanted to lay my agenda down and help her with what she needed. This was not an easy thing for me. I have always enjoyed being in control of everything and now I had to turn my marriage over to God. I had to tell him that Alice was his and my marriage was in his hands. The hardest part is that I had to believe it as well as speak it. It did take the Lord some time to clean up the mess Alice and I had created, but it did not take five years. Within two years we had a love for each other stronger than we ever knew existed. Slowly the Lord was bringing me to a place where I believed there was nothing impossible with Him. Or I will say it another way, that with God all things are possible! **(Matthew 19:26)** This was a display of the triumphant faith I have in the Lord! I was able to step aside and put this difficult situation in his hands.

The second thing that I asked the Lord to fix was my lust problem. This was the one thing I believed He could not fix. I had always had issues with lust. The problem in this area started when I was about 15 years old. I had started to watch XXX pornographic movies at this age. I had lost my virginity at 14 so there was no surprise that I was watching pornographic movies. When I was 16 years old I was introduced to the world of topless bars and strip clubs. I was hanging out with older people at this time who introduced me to this world. This was the start of a 17 year downward spiral. I looked older as I was able to grow facial hair and had no problem getting into strip clubs when I was 16 years old. I did not even get asked for identification. Add to the mix that I was drinking alcohol and doing drugs at this time, which was a risky combination.

By the time I was in my 30's this had gotten progressively worse. I even thought it was OK as a married Christian man to still spend time in the strip clubs. It's NOT! I justified it by saying that I was just looking. I was really lying to myself as I continued to try and convince myself it was OK.

> **1 John 2:16** (NKJV) 16 For all that is in the world—the lust of the flesh, the lust of the eyes, and the pride of life—is not of the Father but is of the world.

Needless to say, the Lord truly went to work on this area of my heart.

The Lord asked me to stay away from these bars and clubs for 30 days and allow Him to work. This was really hard for me because I was on business trips to areas which had clubs I wanted to go to. The temptations were great, but I was obedient to the Lord and stayed away from the clubs for 30 days. At the end of the 30 day period, I felt no desire to walk back in any one of these places again and have not walked in one since. Had I not trusted the Lord, my wife would have most likely left me. Too often this is a matter that is taken too lightly and not addressed. I thank the Lord that He sent me wonderful accountability partners to help me walk this out and make it to the other side. Do not minimize this issue.

Lust is something the enemy uses to completely derail us from our walk with God. It's also a tool the enemy uses to keep us from answering our call to lead our families and to keep us from answering the call of God on our lives. Unfortunately, it's also a tool the enemy uses to tear down Godly men and destroy their marriages and their ministries. It took a triumphant faith to be able to lay lust at the feet of the Lord. I am so thankful I did, because this was an addiction that I struggled with for most of my adult life before I found the Lord. If you are struggling with lust I encourage you to leave it at the feet of Jesus.

The third thing I asked the Lord to fix was my poker and gambling addiction. I had been introduced to Texas Hold'em poker in 2003. I had started playing it once a month with a couple of guys I knew from work. We played what I thought was a harmless $50.00 game. Well it went from once a month to once a week. Then we started to move into $100.00 games. I was winning quite often. I had learned how to play the game and knew how to read people and watch their facial expressions. Of course at this point I was not using these gifts for God, I was using it to further myself. At one point, I was playing three to four evenings per week and neglecting my wife. I was playing all over Florida and in Las Vegas as well. I played with some high end players and held my own. I had an envelope with lots of cash in it that I had from all my winnings. Remember I was still trying to find happiness in people, places, material objects, and money.

Matthew 6:24 (NKJV) 24 "No one can serve two masters; for either he will hate the one and love the other, or else he will be loyal to the one and despise the other. You cannot serve God and mammon.

Shortly after I got saved, a Christian brother of mine sat me down and we had a talk about my poker playing. My excuse or justification was that the people I was playing with were grown men and knew what they were doing. What an excuse! It was an excuse but also not entirely true. Most of the people who ended up playing were degenerate gamblers. They did not have the money to be playing. They were borrowing money, stealing it, or robbing it from others. It would take a while for God to convict me about what I was doing. Every time the Lord tried to show me something about how damaging it was, I would not listen. It took one year after my salvation for me to finally trust the Lord and walk away from this. You see God was refining me and readying me for the call to ministry that would come. I could not see this at the time, but later would understand why things happened the way they did. At first when I stopped playing I felt empty. I felt alone, which I really do not understand today, because it was extremely lonely playing poker with drunken gamblers who could not even sit up straight. I never knew why I enjoyed taking their money so bad. I believe it had to do with the fact I was hurting so much and had such an orphan spirit and was so wounded, that hurting others made me feel good. There is a saying that, "Hurt People, Hurt People." When you are hurting you want others to hurt just like you and feel the same pain you're feeling. I had such strong temptations after I stopped playing to go play again. The only one who could heal me of those was Jesus. **Hebrews 2:18** (NKJV) 18 For in that He Himself has suffered, being tempted, He is able to aid those who are tempted.

I was so thankful I had Christian brothers to walk with at this time to help lead me to a place of repentance. Repentance was one of the hardest things I had to do, but is one of the foundations of my walk with the Lord today.

> **Luke 5:31-32** (NKJV) 31 Jesus answered and said to them, "Those who are well have no need of a physician, but those who are sick. 32 I have not come to call *the* righteous, but sinners, to repentance."

A complete walk in triumphant faith took place as I trusted the Lord to lift the gambling addiction from me. I hope you are starting to see by now, that we must have a triumphant faith. We need to have faith like that of David. David's faith took him through his battle with Goliath. David's faith in the Lord allowed him to kill giants.

The fourth thing I asked the Lord to fix was my housing situation. My wife and I bought a house in 2003 together. This house was purchased at a great price and was supposed to be something we could afford. Instead, we simply did not how to live within our means and kept running up credit card bills and living at a level that was 20% higher than the money we were bringing in. We were not good stewards of our money. So about every two years, as our house gained value, we would take out a second mortgage against our house or refinance our house and pull more cash out to pay our bills. In 2009 God finally stopped the madness. He spoke so clearly to us about living on cash and working to pay off all of our debts. I was horrified at the thought of having to cut our lifestyle and the way we had been living. Little did I know God was up to something supernatural to teach my wife and me about who

He was. We started tithing around this time and the first month we tithed, we were going to be short $1,800.00 on our bills because of our tithe. Miraculously all of our bills were paid that month. We watched as the Lord gave us abundance in our finances. We did walk through some lessons and learn some things, but it seemed to be painless for us. I remember a scripture that God told us to test him in regards to finances. It's the only scripture that God challenges us to test him.

Malachi 3:10-11 (NKJV) 10 Bring all the tithes into the storehouse, That there may be food in My house, And try Me now in this," Says the Lord of hosts, "If I will not open for you the windows of heaven And pour out for you *such* blessing That *there will* not *be room* enough *to receive it.* 11 "And I will rebuke the devourer for your sakes, So that he will not destroy the fruit of your ground, Nor shall the vine fail to bear fruit for you in the field," Says the Lord of hosts;

We continued to be faithful to the Lord on this. The next thing we knew we were living on less money than we had ever lived on before, and were living in his abundance. This was a huge sign for us that God was rewarding our obedience for our giving. I was a skeptic about tithes and offerings. I was someone who did not believe in this at all. Then I heard the scripture in Malachi 3:10-11 and I figured I better test God. This required triumphant faith to stick to what the Lord had requested of us. There were many weeks I did not want to give, and I did not want to trust the Lord with our finances, but we knew we must continue to do this. After we had been tithing for two and a half years the Lord released his blessings over us, and we were able to get our mortgage modified. This did not come easy at all. There were months of back and forth with the bank on this, and often times we felt that we were not going to get the loan modified. So God sent us an attorney friend to help us through this. She did not even charge us. Thank you Jesus! This was a real life lesson in triumphant faith. My wife and I had to have faith like David's to make it through this time.

    The fifth and final area the Lord fixed was my morbid obesity. Over the years I had put on 170 pounds in a ten year period. I was the heaviest I had ever been in my life. It was hurting my back and my knees as well. God used things to show me it was time to turn this over to him. One of the signs was that when I ministered one night for one hour, and then prayed over people for another 30 minutes. I was so winded by the time I got done that I had to go have some Gatorade. Another sign the Lord showed me was that I gained eight pounds in one month. The biggest thing the Lord used to show me that this was a serious issue that must be laid at his feet, was when I had a dream one night. In this dream I was walking down the street and I was 500 pounds and had a heart attack and fell to the ground. Before I could get my cell phone out to call 911, I died right there on the sidewalk. This dream scared me enough to force me into looking into lap band surgery. I had been talking about the lap band for ten years but had never gotten serious about it. At this time, the Lord blessed my wife and with some unexpected money, and we were able to use it to pay for my surgery. I went and met with the doctor and knew that this was the Lord calling me to have this surgery. I had a wonderful doctor and a great team that helped me through the pre-surgery period of liquid fasting, the surgery, and the post-surgery period. I see my doctor every month to help keep me accountable and make sure I am staying on track. At this time I am down 100 pounds and living a healthy lifestyle once again. Thank You Jesus! Triumphant faith was such a strong part of this equation.

    So often the world sees a shepherd boy, but God sees a King. As you just read, the Lord fixed all five of these things in five years. Just as He promised He would. He did these in His time, not mine. I had to have David's kind of triumphant faith to get through this time period. Many of us are not prepared to wait a week for God to do something, let alone five years. I want to encourage you that God chose you and called you to live a life together with Him. Not apart from Him, but with Him. Give the Lord a chance to move in your life and in your circumstances. I promise you that if you will submit to Him and lay your problems at His feet, you will not be disappointed.

Triumphant Faith

12: The Benjamin Blessing

In September of 2011, I started learning about Benjamin. Through a series of teachings I started to understand the anointing of Benjamin. During this time period the Lord used this teaching to speak to me. You have read the previous 11 chapters not knowing that my name is Benjamin. When you are born in the Jewish faith you are given a Hebrew name at birth. Most always you are named after someone who is no longer living. You are named in remembrance of that person. As for me, Benjamin (or Ben as he was called) is my mom's father who I never met, because he died two years before I was born. Ben was the first husband of my Nana Sadie. So my parents named me Ben-Zion. The English name they gave me was Bradley Carl Gillman.

In December of 2011, the Lord spoke the name Benjamin over me once again. He told me that he bestowed a Benjamin anointing on me. He told me that 2012 would be my breakthrough year in life. He told me that in 2012 I would have the full anointing of Benjamin on me. Some of you would like to know what that means? Well I am going to tell you.

The Benjamin Blessing

Genesis 43:34 (NKJV) 34 Then he took servings to them from before him, but Benjamin's serving was five times as much as any of theirs. So they drank and were merry with him.

That's right! Benjamin's anointing is five times that of his brothers. It's been prophesied that 2012 is the year of the Benjamin anointing. Benjamin is the 12th son of the 12 tribes of Israel. This book is 12 chapters long, and is being written in 2012. I had originally planned for ten chapters in this book, and now we are having 12. At 12:01 on January 1, 2012, I felt such a strong move of the Holy Ghost come over me, and right at that moment, I knew this would be a year of five times the blessings.

I started to write this book in November of 2011. I wrote about six pages and could not get any further. I prayed about it and listened for the voice of God about when to continue and heard nothing. In December I had two and half weeks off of work, and thought I was going to write again. Once again, nothing came from my heart to write. I was calling out to the Lord asking him how I was going to finish this book by June first if I had not even started to write in December. During this period of time I fasted for 21 days from food, and was only on liquids. When the fast was over the Lord spoke two things to me. The first was that His love for me was not performance based. Second was that it was time for me to rest and He would tell me when it was time to write the book. So I spent December resting and receiving from the Lord. I came into January and was raring to go on writing the book, but I was still not able to write. January through June has traditionally been my busy season at work. January started off very busy and I was working a lot. My birthday was January 13th and I decided to go to a healing service about an hour away from our house. Many things happened that night, but most importantly a healing began in my heart. My body had been healed in December and now my heart was getting healed. Two weeks later my wife and I had an opportunity to go to a conference in Tampa to hear Apostle Joshua Fowler and Apostle John Eckhardt preach. We were not going to go, but the Lord spoke for us to go over to this conference. Apostle Eckhardt preached on "Sonship," and it really ministered to me. I realized I had been a son of God the whole time, and I still thought I needed to earn it. It brought confirmation to what the Lord had spoken over me in December. Apostle Fowler preached on the Benjamin Blessing. Now this was the third time I had heard him preach this same message in three weeks. It's funny how my flesh was telling me that I did not need to hear this message again, but the Lord had other plans. This word was for me. I needed to hear it three times. I actually got the CD and listened to it two more times for a total of five. After this weekend, I was excited and wanted to write my book. I went to sit down one night in late January to write, and the Lord still would not let me write this book.

In February I was all ready to write the book, and the Lord would have other plans. Apostle Fowler was holding a boot camp called "School of the Apostles and Prophets" every Saturday in February. At that point the Lord spoke to me and told me that I would not be able to write this book until after the boot camp. My wife and I attended the boot camp and it was amazing the things the Lord imparted into me. It was an awesome four weeks of teaching, preaching, and prophesying and I learned so much. So God imparted a Benjamin anointing on me in December. I got healing, deliverance, and impartation in January. I got teaching in February, and now I was ready to write the book - so I thought!

I was about to take a trip out to California and Las Vegas. I was going to California for vacation and Las Vegas for work. My wife was coming with me and we were headed out there from March 2 - March 12. I figured God was doing this so I could start writing March 2nd. I was wrong once again. Have you seen the pattern? Every time I try to impose my will, the Lord steps in and puts His will into place.

Matthew 6:7-10 (NKJV) 7 And when you pray, do not use vain repetitions as the heathen *do*. For they think that they will be heard for their many words. 8 "Therefore do not be like them. For your Father knows the things you have need of before you ask Him. 9 In this manner, therefore, pray: Our Father in heaven, Hallowed be Your name. 10 Your kingdom come. Your will be done on earth as it is in heaven.

The word from the Lord on March 1 was for me to rest until March 15th and then I would be able to start writing this book. I complained to the Lord that 75 days was not enough time to write 12 chapters. The Lord just laughed and told me he could have me write the whole book in three days and to rest and know that He is God. So I did!

March 15th I started writing the book. It took me 30 days to write the first two chapters. After that I wrote the next ten chapters over the next 30 days. **Philippians 4:13** (NKJV) 13 I can do all things through Christ who strengthens me.

I have not forced any chapter in this book at all. Every time I have written it has been ordained by God to write on that evening. I have learned much about myself as I have written this book. More importantly I have learned more about who God is and how He will reveal himself to you. This year has been a year of five times anointing over my life. This has been the most fruitful year of my life to this point, and the best part is I know God has so much more for me. I wanted to share about the writing of this book with you to encourage you. I want to tell you that, "Yes, you *can* do it!" You can do whatever God has called you to. It all starts with finding out what the call on your life is.

I never grew up wanting to write books. More importantly, English was never one of my best subjects in school. In fact, I did not like it at all. I took a journalism class in college and dreaded going to the class every week. Something happened to me to get to the point to write a book. God showed me what He had called me to do. I had to have trust and faith in Him that this is what He had called me to do. The only experience I ever had writing a book previous to this was that I wrote reviews of strip clubs on websites. How awesome is God that He turned me into a man who wrote a book glorifying Jesus as Lord. How awesome is God that in 2004 I tried to burn a Bible, and now the Lord has me sending Spanish Bibles to Central and South America. The Lord took me from being thrust into the fire of hell, to being thrust into fire of God!

Throughout my life, so many people tried to introduce me to Jesus. They did this by condemning me and telling me I was going to hell for my sins. They told me I was going to die in a lake of fire if I did not clean up my act. When I did get saved, I heard a very different story than that. Our faith is based on love. Our Heavenly Father loved us so much that He sent his only begotten son to die for us.

John 3:16 (NKJV) 16 For God so loved the world that He gave His only begotten Son, that whoever believes in Him should not perish but have everlasting life.

Romans 5:8 (NKJV) 8 But God demonstrates His own love toward us, in that while we were still sinners, Christ died for us.

Romans 8:37-39 (NKJV) 37 Yet in all these things we are more than conquerors through Him who loved us. 38 For I am persuaded that neither death nor life, nor angels nor principalities nor powers, nor things present nor things to come, 39 nor height nor depth, nor any other created thing, shall be able to separate us from the love of God which is in Christ Jesus our Lord.

Galatians 2:20 (NKJV) 20 I have been crucified with Christ; it is no longer I who live, but Christ lives in me; and the *life* which I now live in the flesh I live by faith in the Son of God, who loved me and gave Himself for me.

It's the love of our Heavenly Father that will bring many to Jesus. I want to encourage you when you are sharing Jesus with someone that you need to share the love of Jesus with them. Early on in ministry I use to preach with a spirit of condemnation on me and tried to scare people into salvation. As I grew in the Lord I stopped dwelling on where we are going to spend eternity and started focusing on how we are going to live the rest of our lives. I focus today on what Jesus can do for you right now in this place. I have seen miracles, signs, and wonders throughout my walk with the Lord and witnessed the life changing power of Jesus Christ in my own life and the lives of others. Some days are not easy, but at least I have Jesus walking hand in hand with me.

I want to thank you for reading this story of how the Lord changed me. I pray that you will allow God to move in your life in the way that He has moved in mine. I hope you are encouraged to seek the Lord in everything you do! Always know that you have hope in Jesus Christ and that God is the same yesterday, today, and forever. He has not forgotten about you! Allow Jesus to take you out of the fire you have been in and thrust you into the fire of His presence! **Hebrews 13:8** (NKJV) 8 Jesus Christ *is* the same yesterday, today, and forever.

I wanted to end this book with something special. I want to speak a "Benjamin Blessing" over you. So please repeat the following:

> "In the name of the Lord Jesus, I speak Benjamin Blessings over all areas of my life. I speak a Benjamin Blessing of five times increase over my finances, marriage, health, employment, ministries, businesses, family, and my heart."

The Benjamin Blessing

As we say at Legacy Life Church in Orlando, FL, "Be blessed, blessed, blessed, blessed, blessed to be a blessing in Jesus name, Amen!"

About The Author

Brad Gillman serves as the President of HSGEM (Hawaiian Shirt Guy Evangelism Ministries) an Itinerant and Missions ministry. In addition, Brad is a Regional Sales Manager and also a business consultant for small to medium sized businesses.

Brad and his wife, Alice, also serve as Deacons at Legacy Life Church in Orlando, FL, under the leadership of Apostles Joshua and Deborah Ashley Fowler.

Brad preaches throughout the United States with boldness and authority. He also sends thousands of Spanish Bibles annually to Central and South America.

Brad is a Born-Again Jewish Believer who has been given powerful gifts to preach, teach, and prophesy and is using them to lead people into the Glorious Light of Jesus Christ! Brad teaches Evangelism Boot Camps that show how to effectively evangelize. He also leads men's fellowship groups and accountability meetings to help educate men about their role in the Kingdom of God. Brad has a heart to see the fatherless restored to their Heavenly Father and to see the Orphan Spirit broken so we can take our place as sons of the Most High God.

Brad resides in Central Florida with the love of his life Alice, and their 2 cats (Oscar and George) and their dog Fred.

To contact Brad Gillman for ministry engagements or resources:

www.hsgem.org
hsgemb@gmail.com
321-578-8620

Thrust Into The Fire

Recommended Reading

Governors Of Praise

Access Granted

ID Required

To order copies visit:
www.legacylife.org
or call
(407) 654-3344

Made in the USA
Charleston, SC
05 August 2012